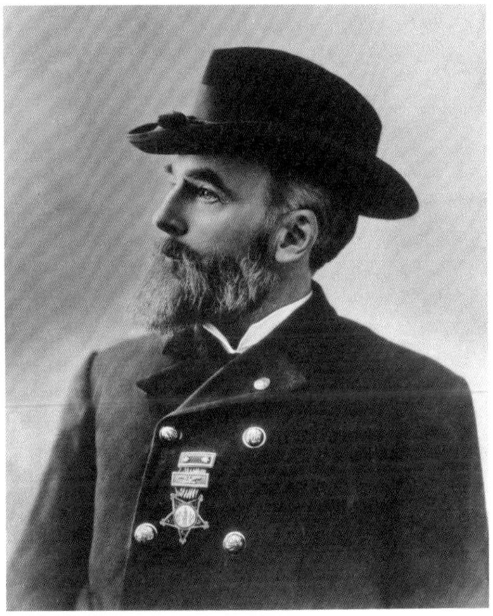

Dwight Divine
c. 1886, Wawarsing, NY

Knives Jason Koxvold

Last Songs
Galway Kinnell

1

What do they sing, the last birds
coasting down the twilight,
banking
across woods filled with darkness, their
frayed wings
curved on the world like a lover's arms
which form, night after night, in sleep,
an irremediable absence?

2

Silence. Ashes
in the grate. Whatever it is
that keeps us from heaven,
sloth, wrath, greed, fear, could we only
reinvent it on earth
as song.

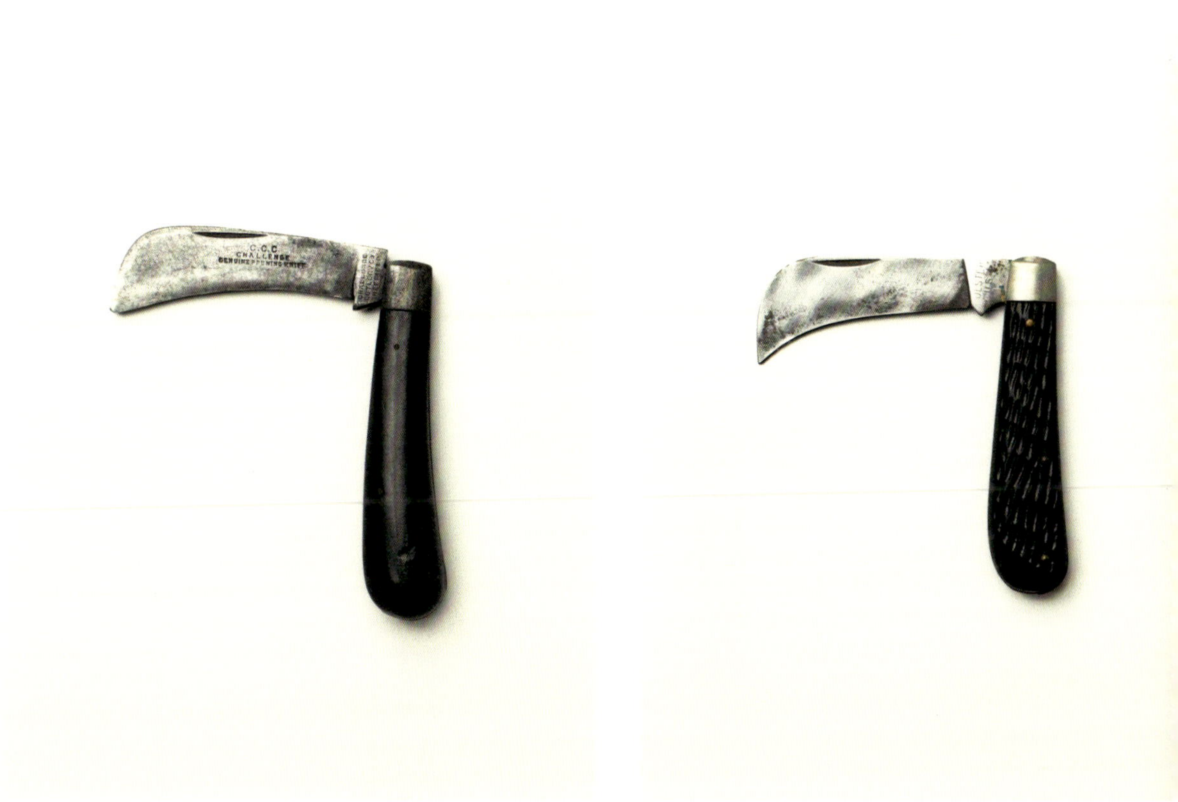

Hawkbill Pruner, Challenge Cutlery Co
c. 1867, Sheffield, UK

Hawkbill Pruner, Ulster Knife Co
c. 1884, Newburgh, NY

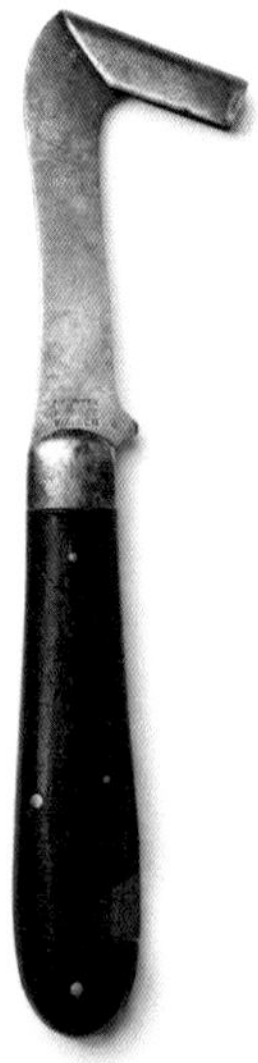

Timber Scribe, New York Knife Co
c. 1895, Walden, NY

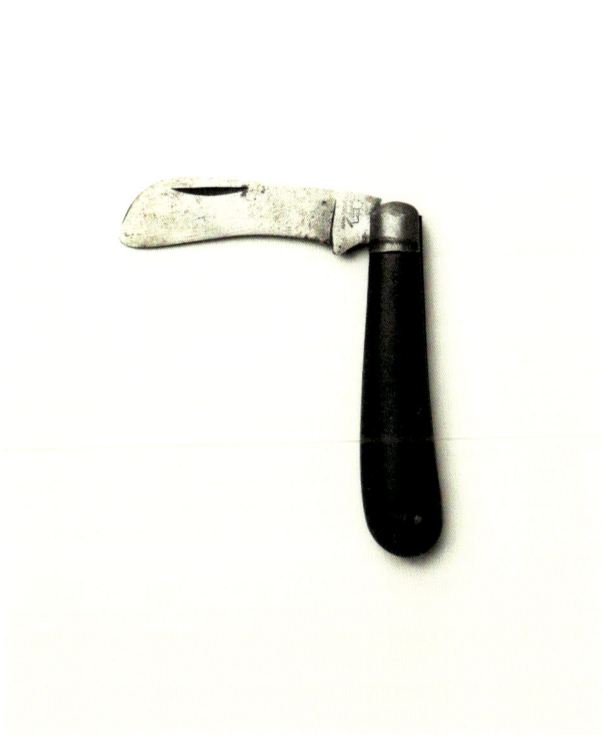

Hawkbill Pruner, Hammer Brand
c. 1897, Walden, NY

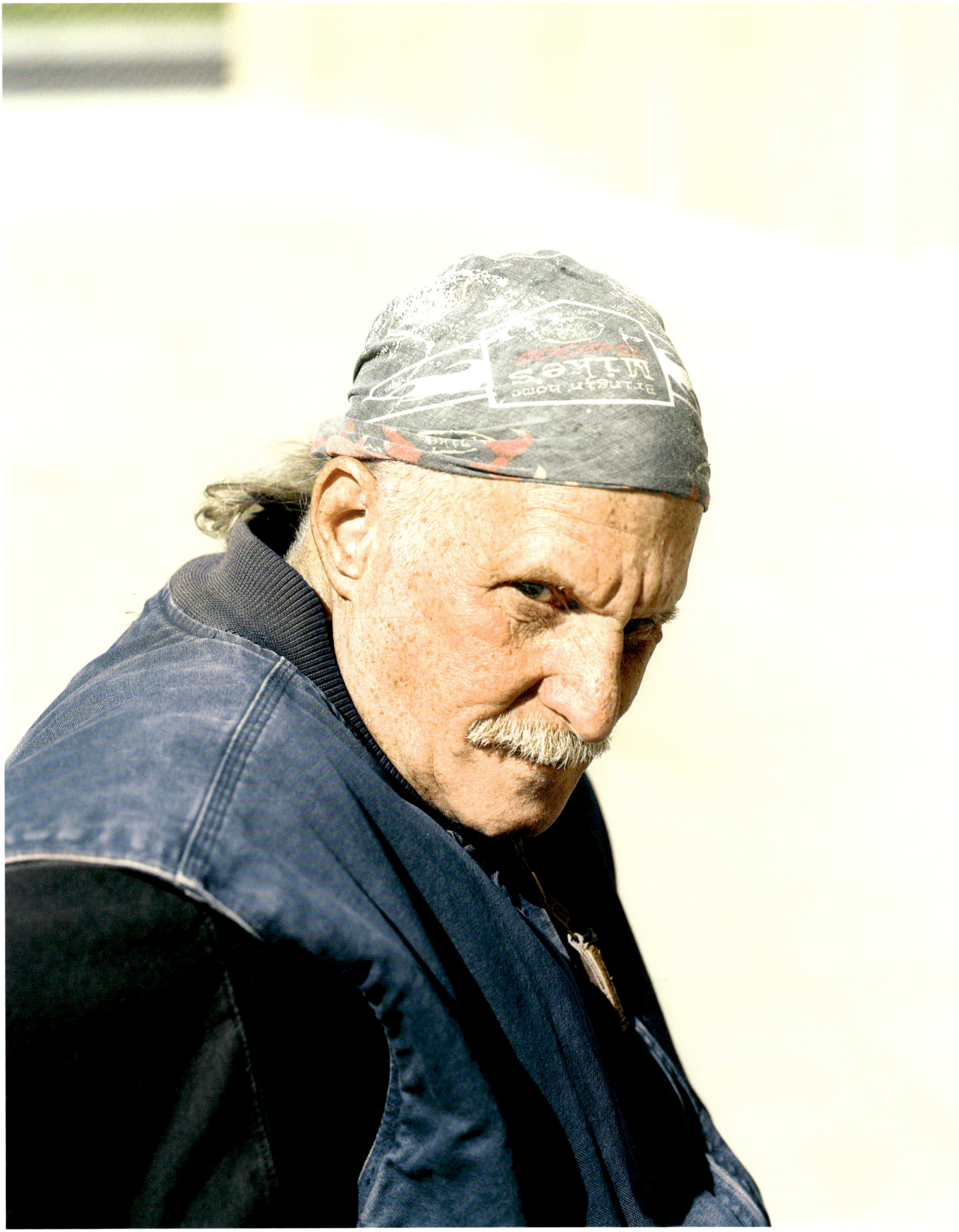
Mike's
Bringin home

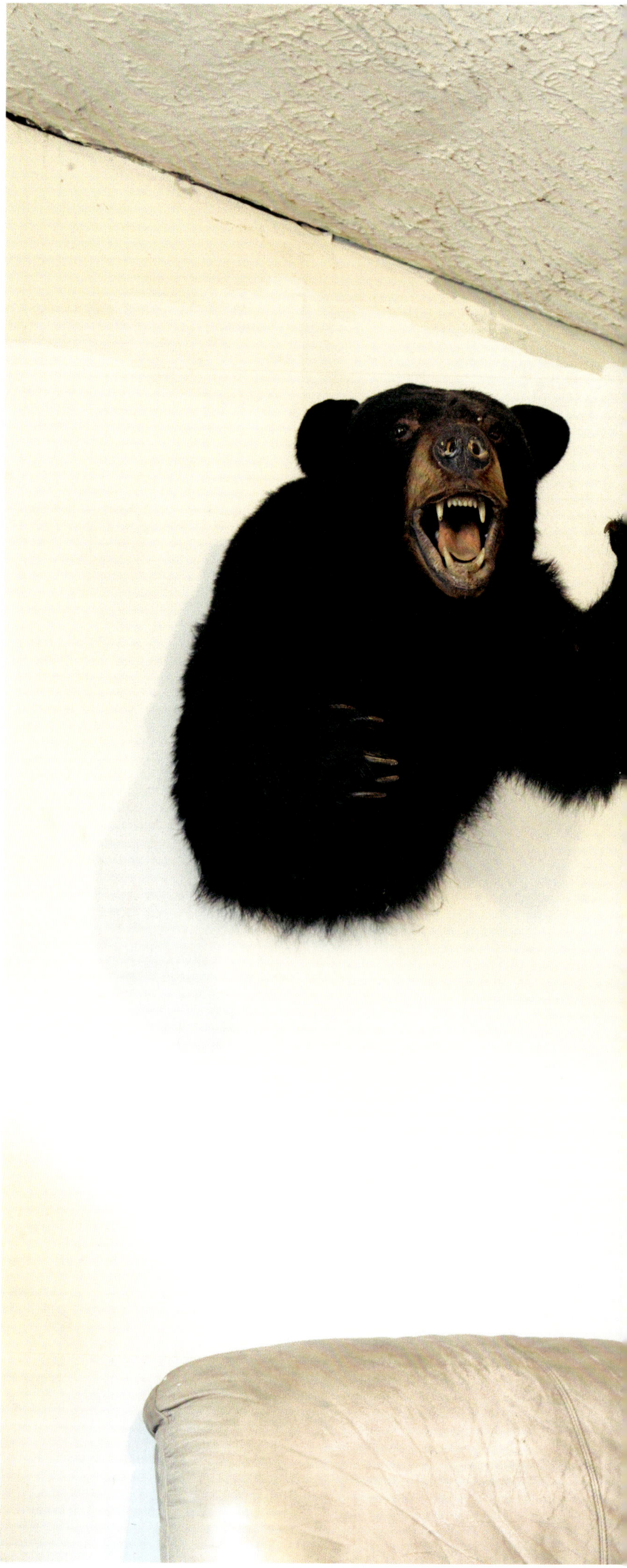

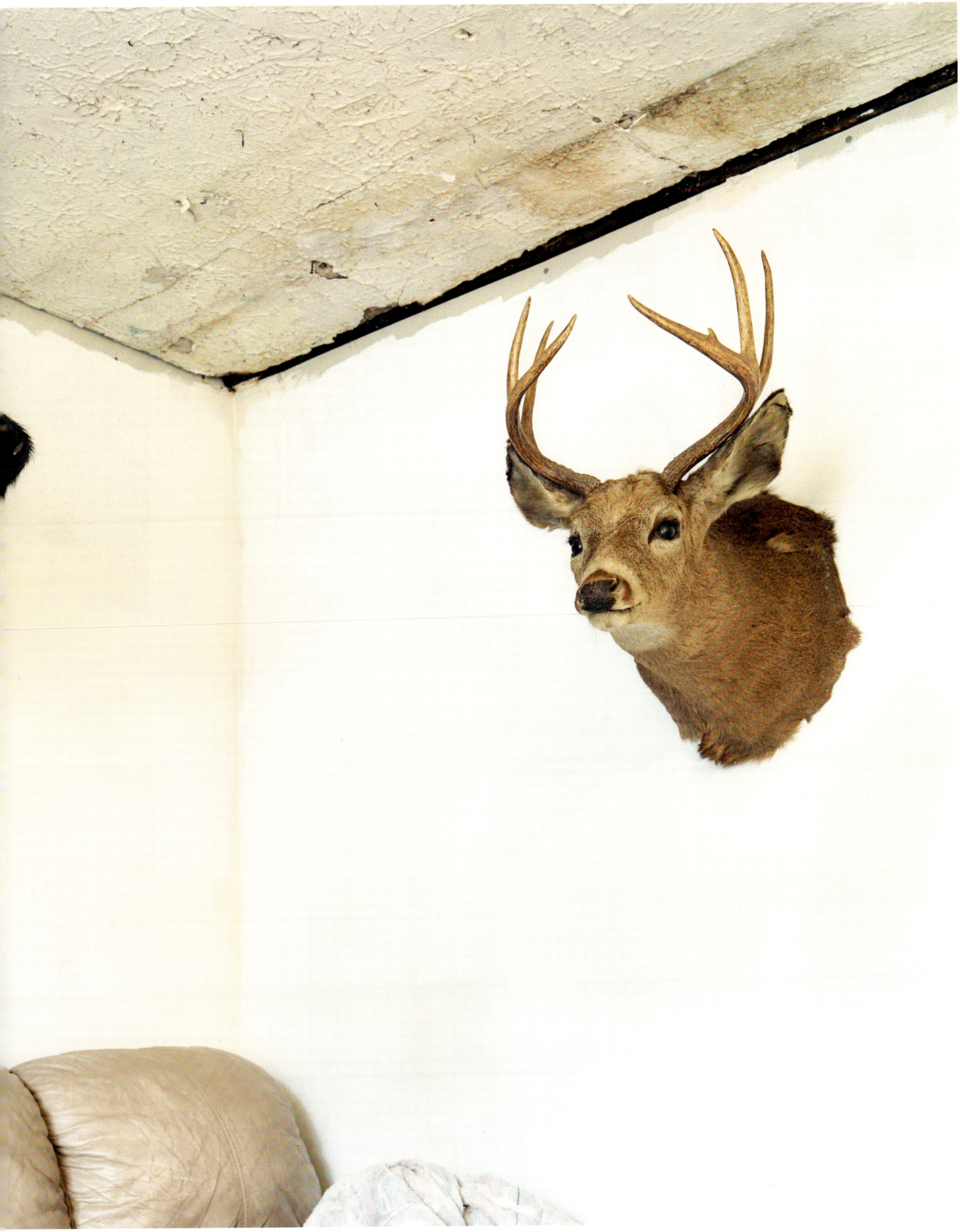

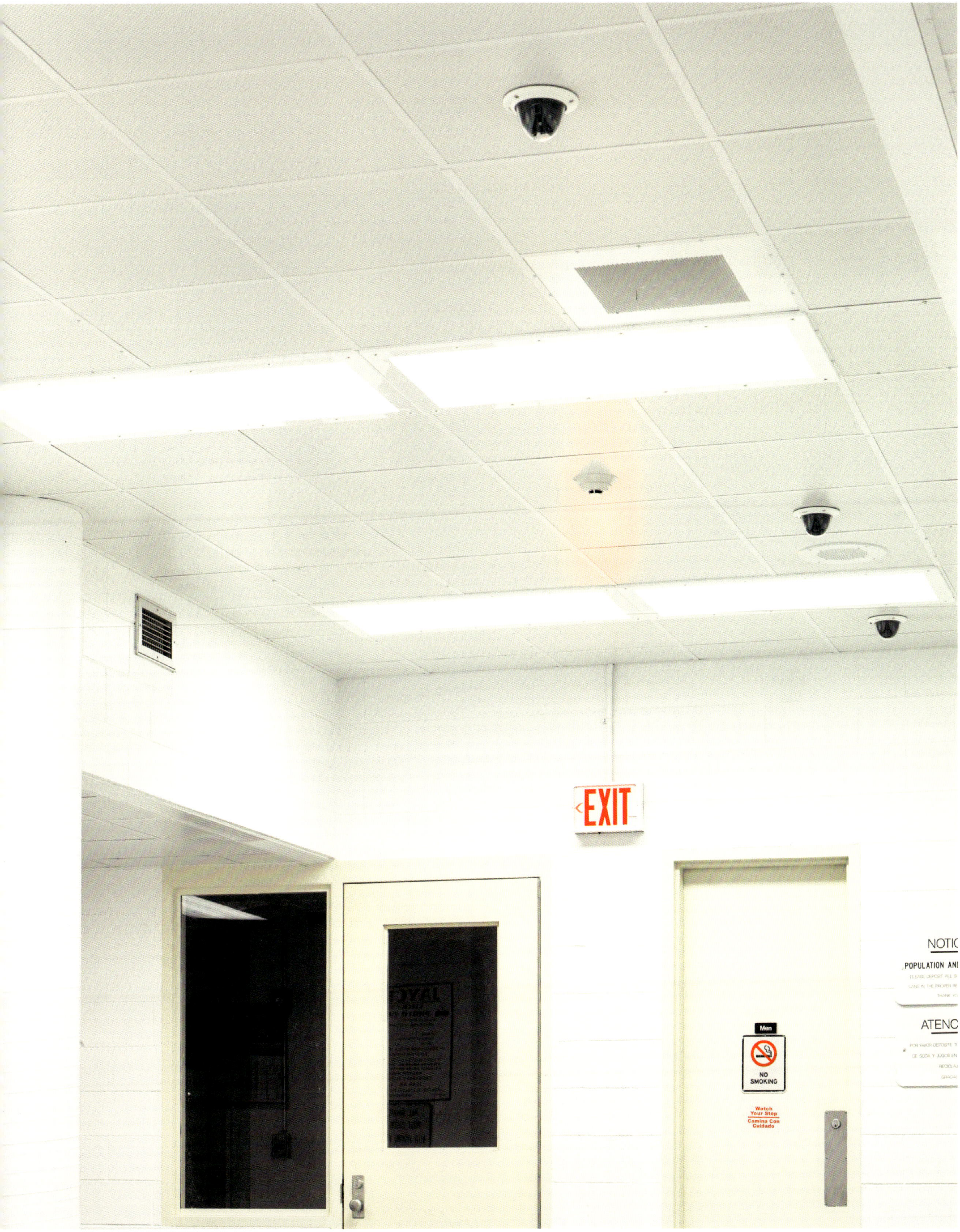
EXIT
NOTIC
POPULATION AN
ATENC
Men
NO SMOKING
Watch Your Step
Camina Con Cuidado

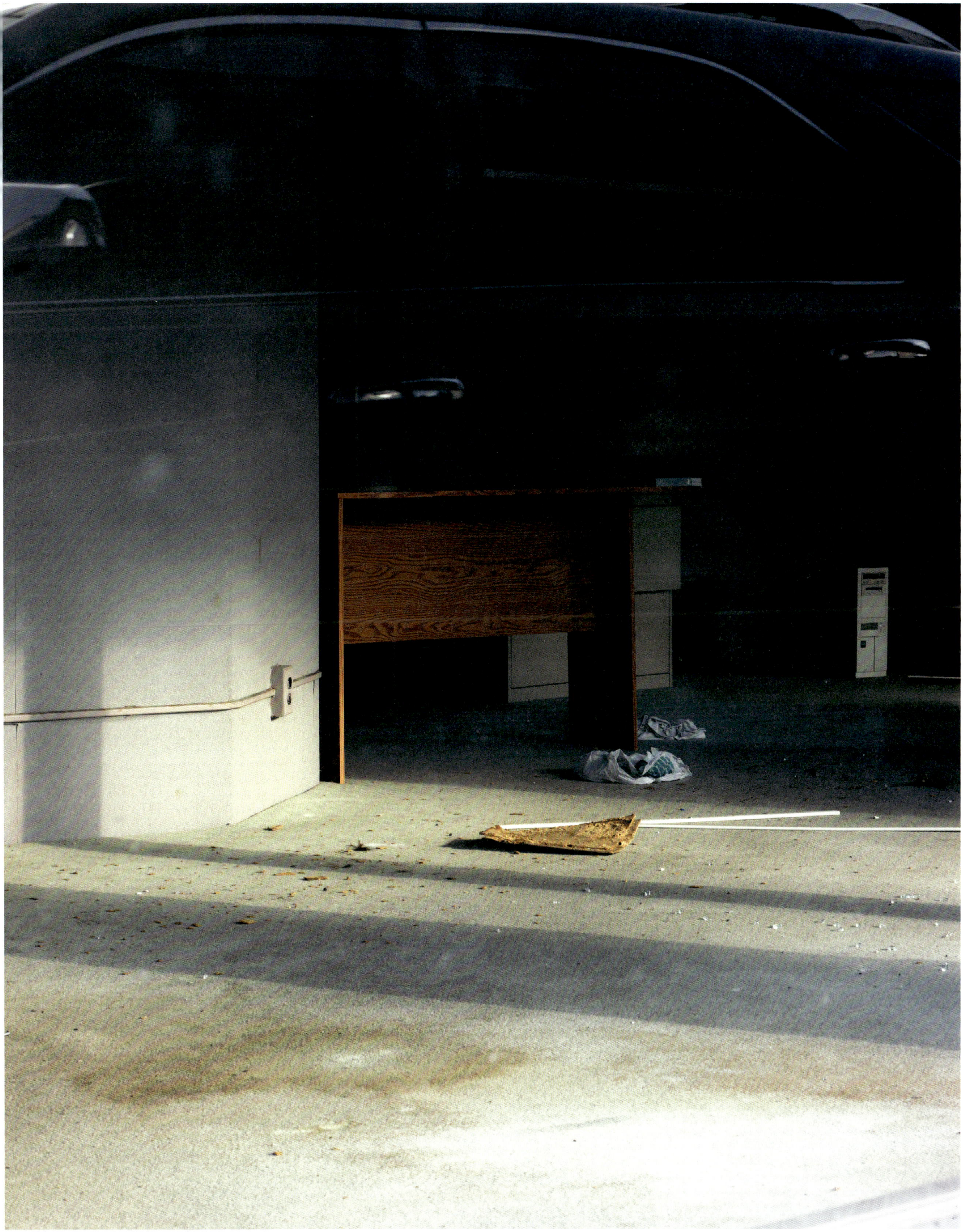

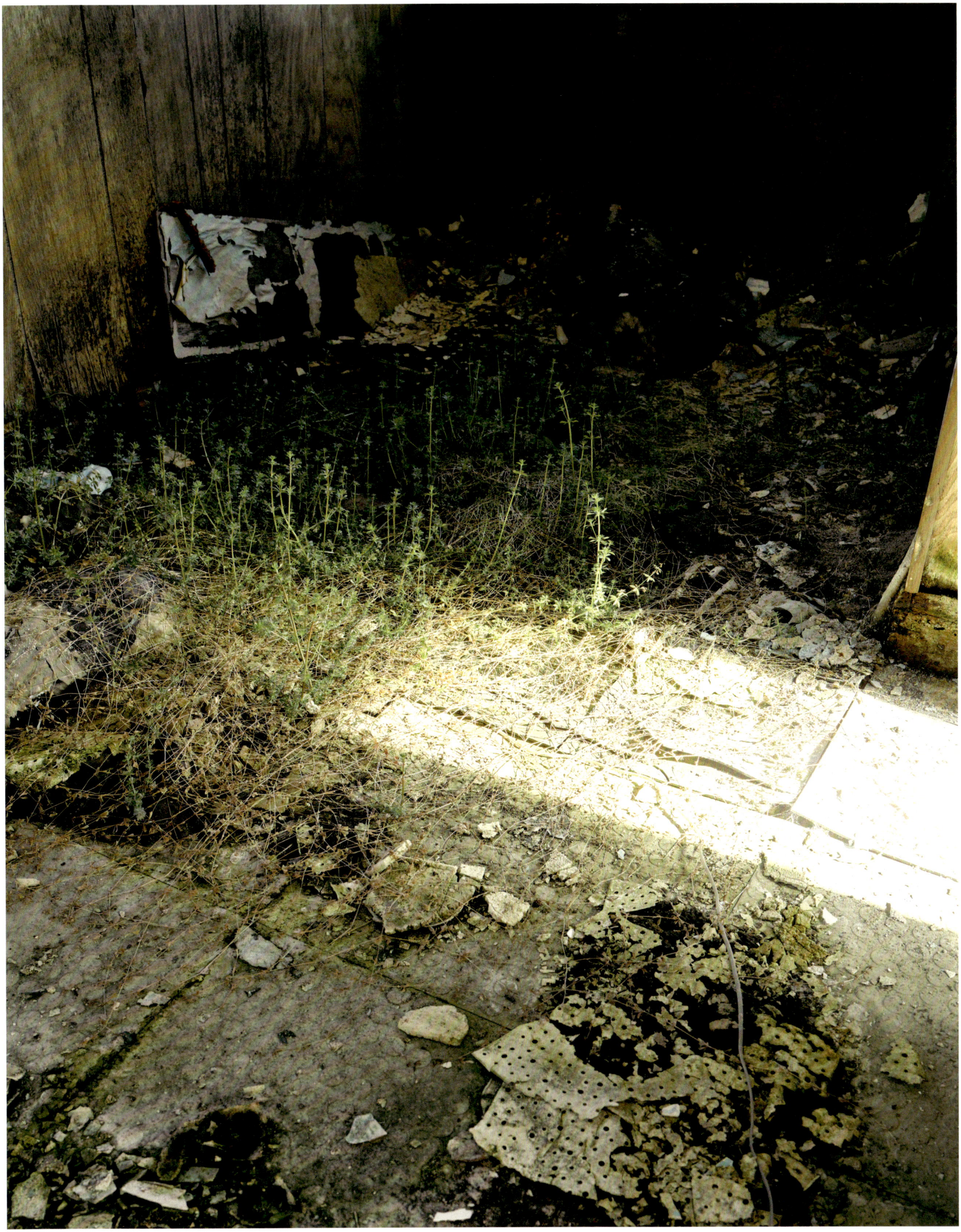

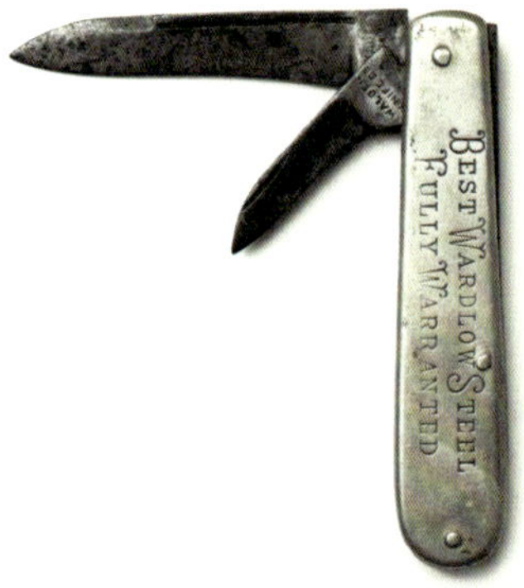

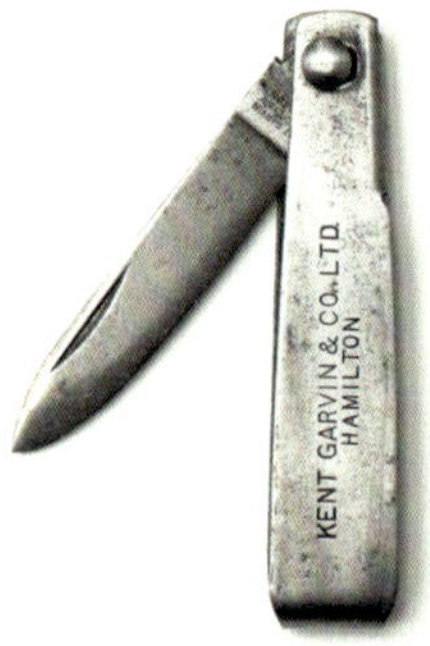

Metal Advertising Knife, Walden Knife Co
c. 1915, Walden, NY

Metal Pocket Knife, Allen Cutlery Co
c. 1921, Newburgh, NY

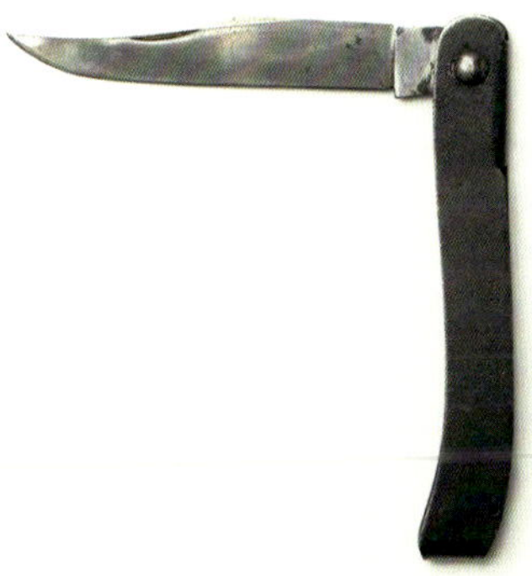

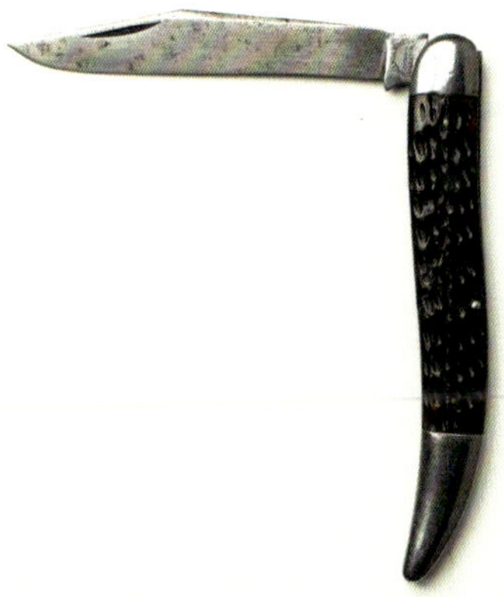

“Nigger Chaser”, Allen Cutlery Co
c. 1923, Newburgh, NY

Jigged Bone Toothpick, Wallkill River Works
c. 1923, Walden, NY

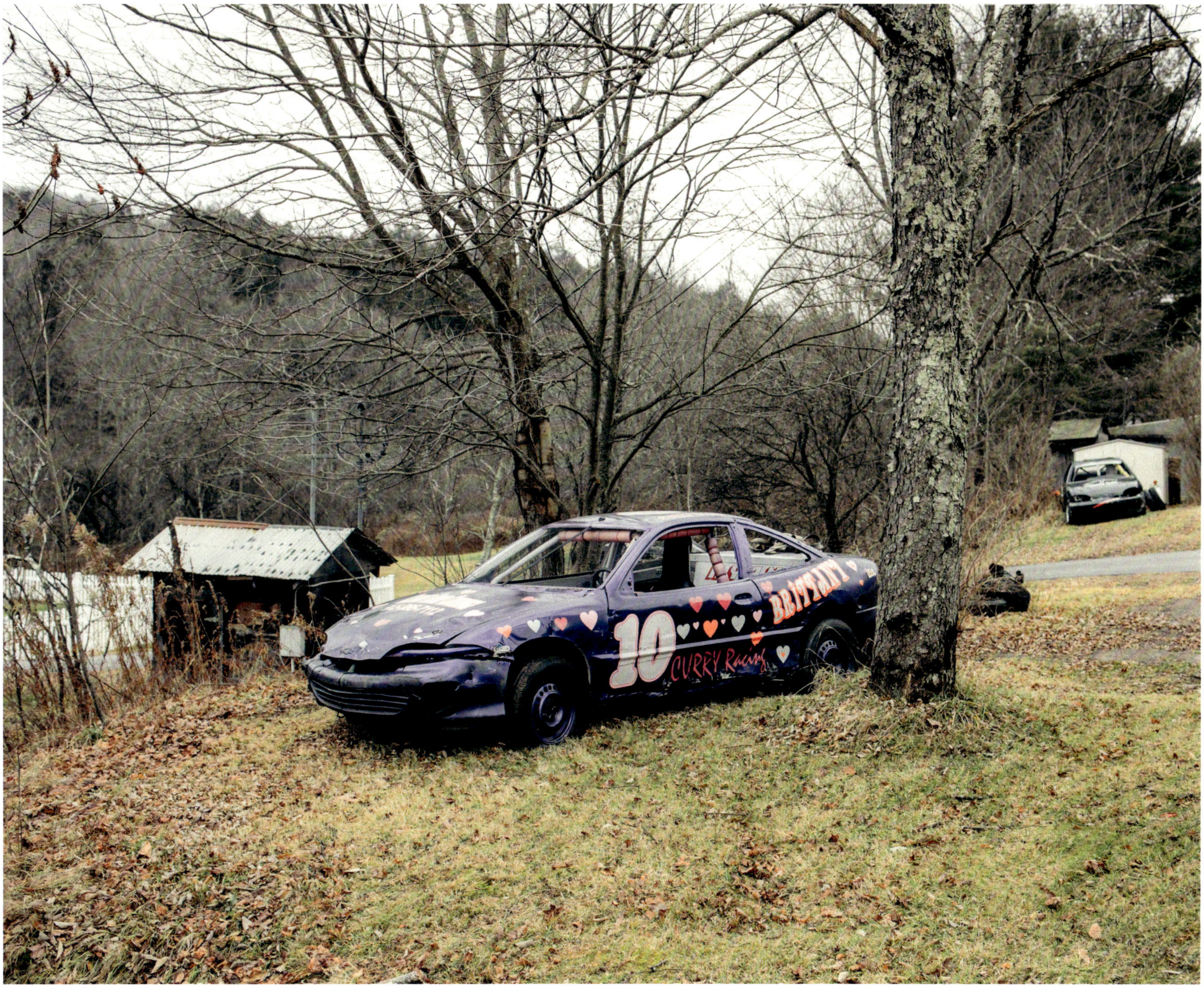
BRITTANY
10
CURRY Racing

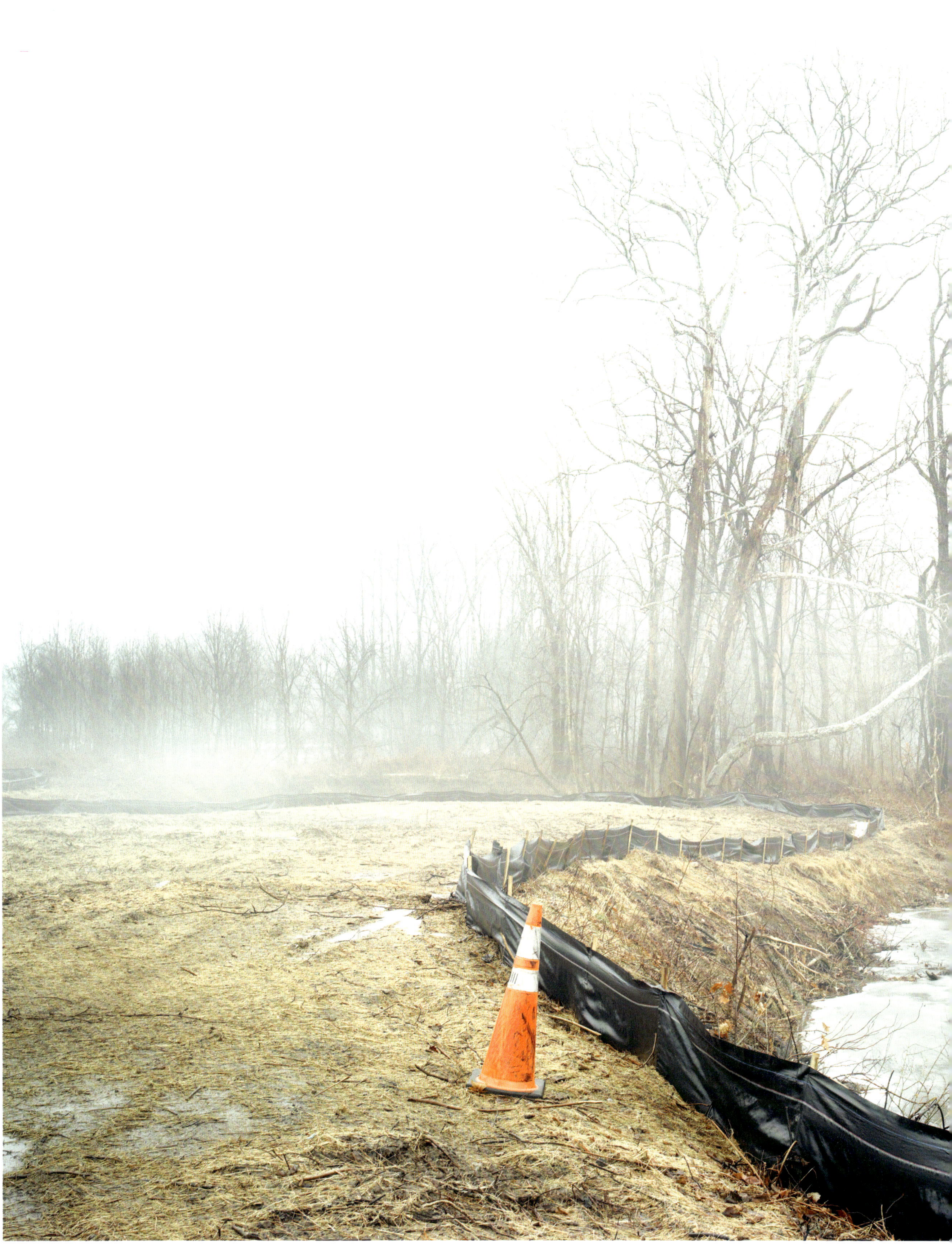

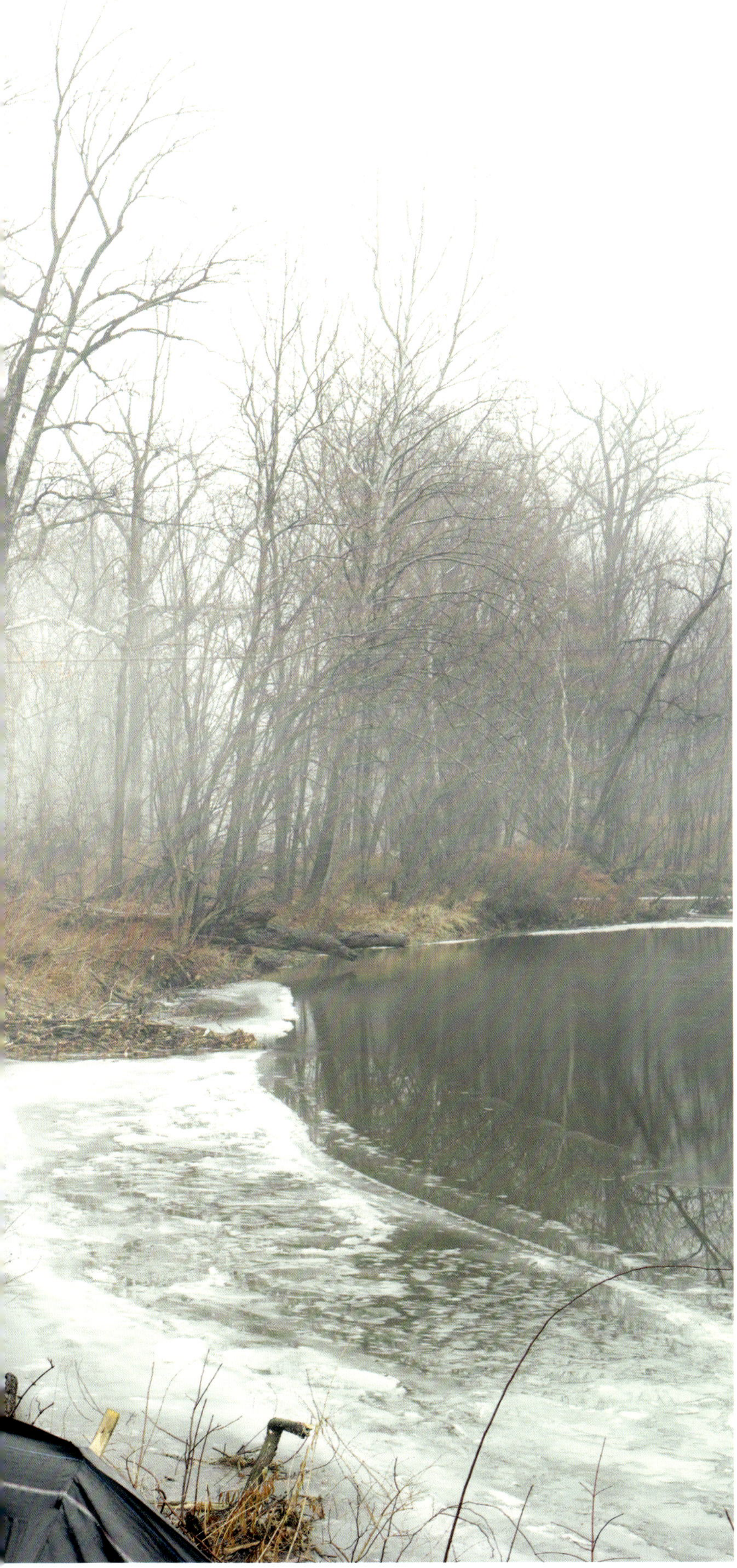

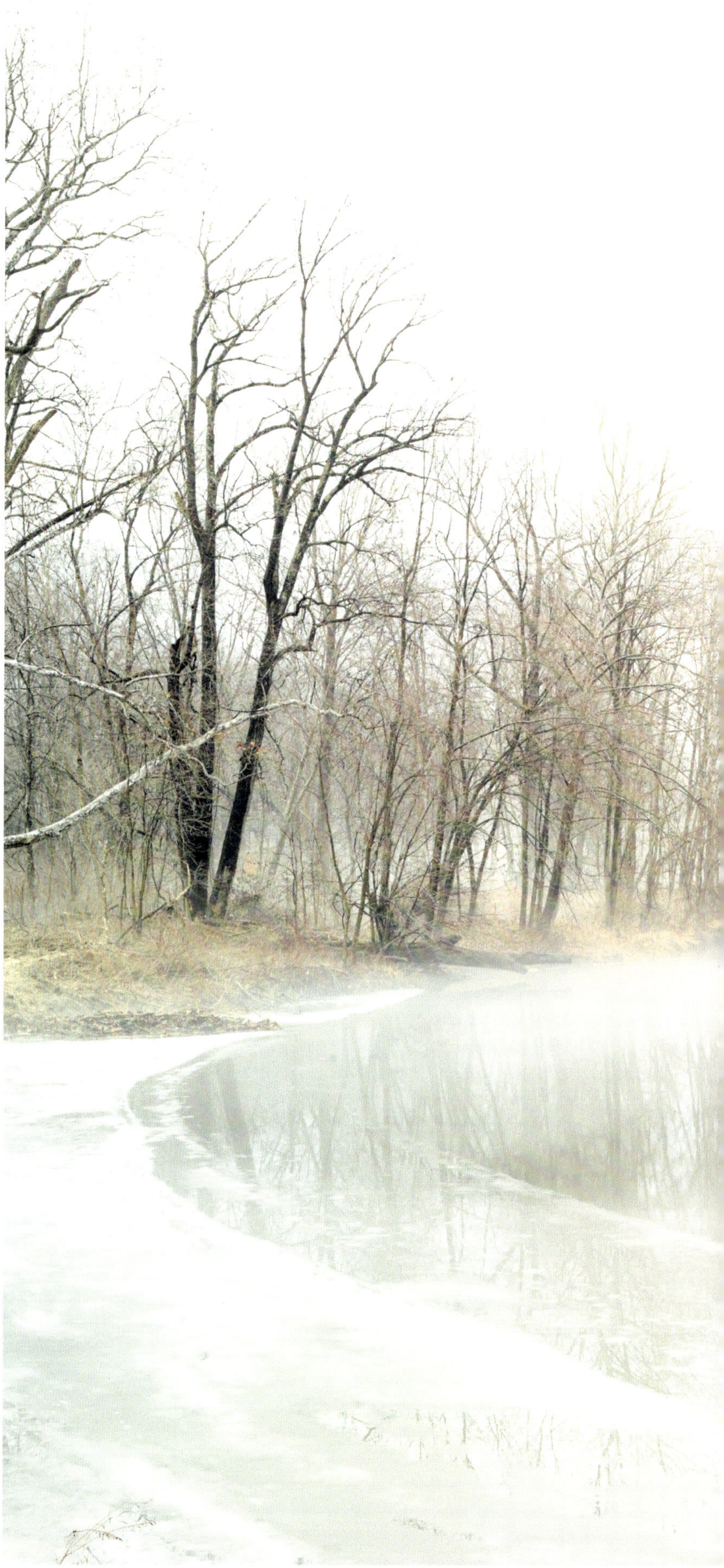

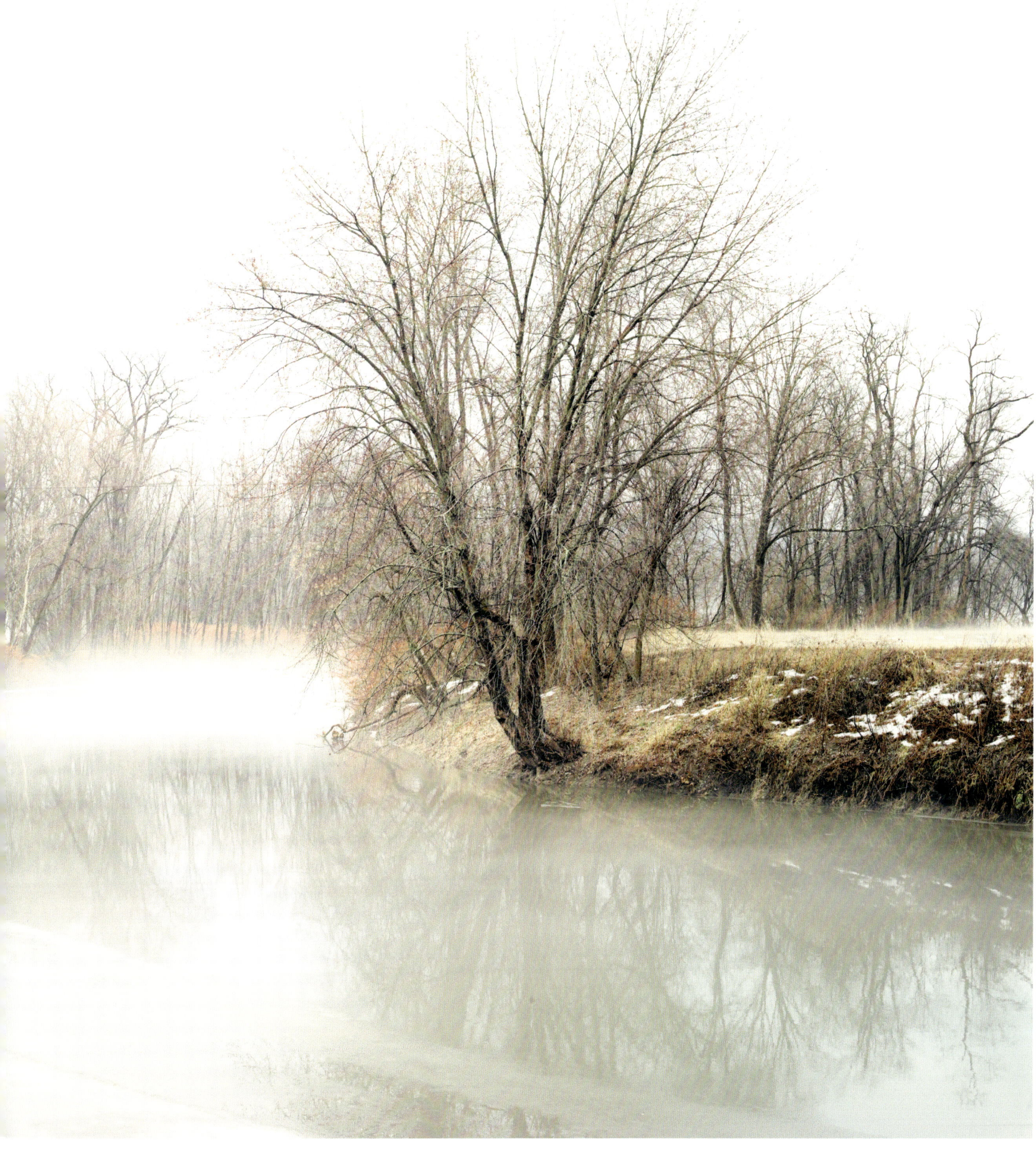

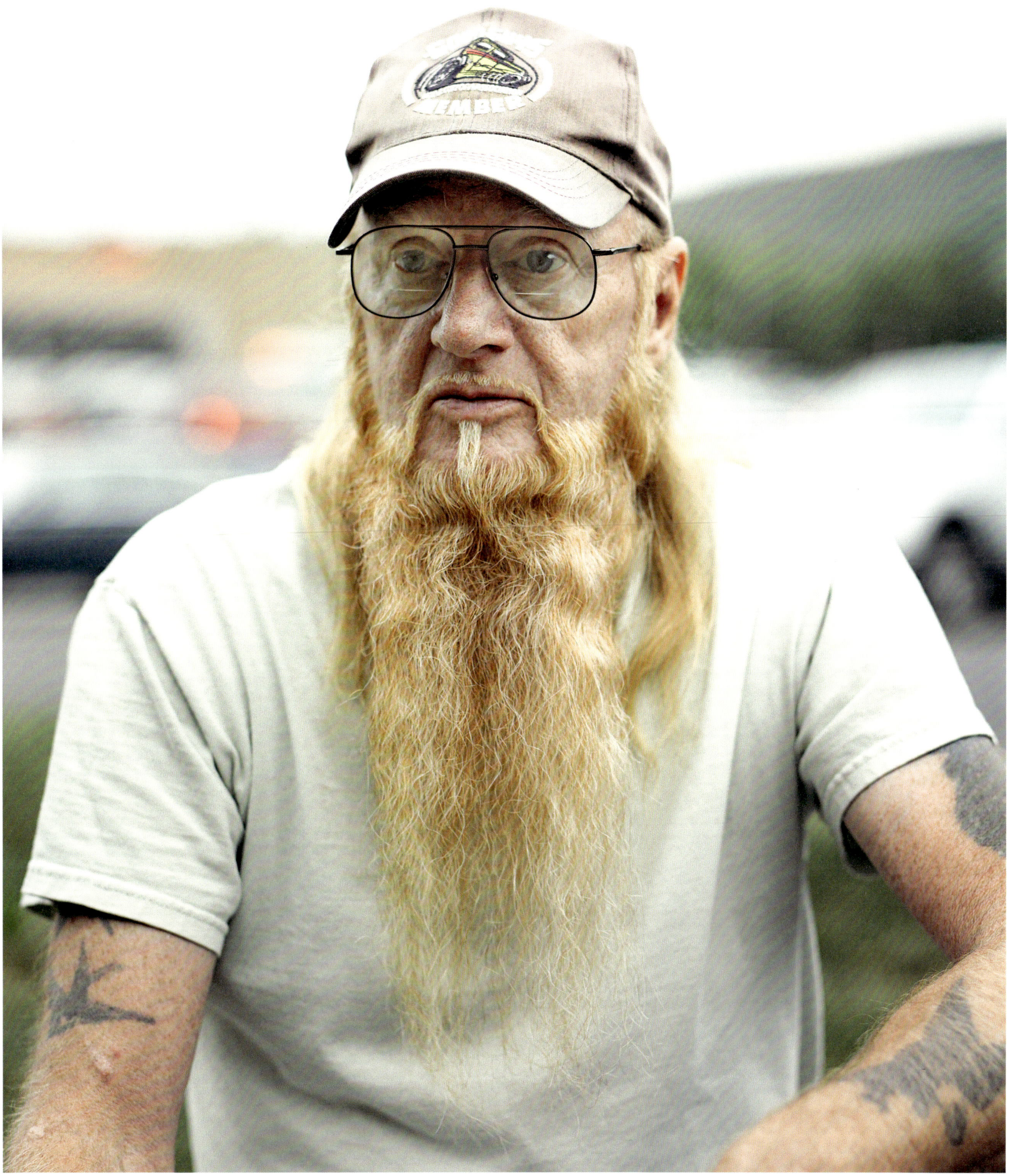

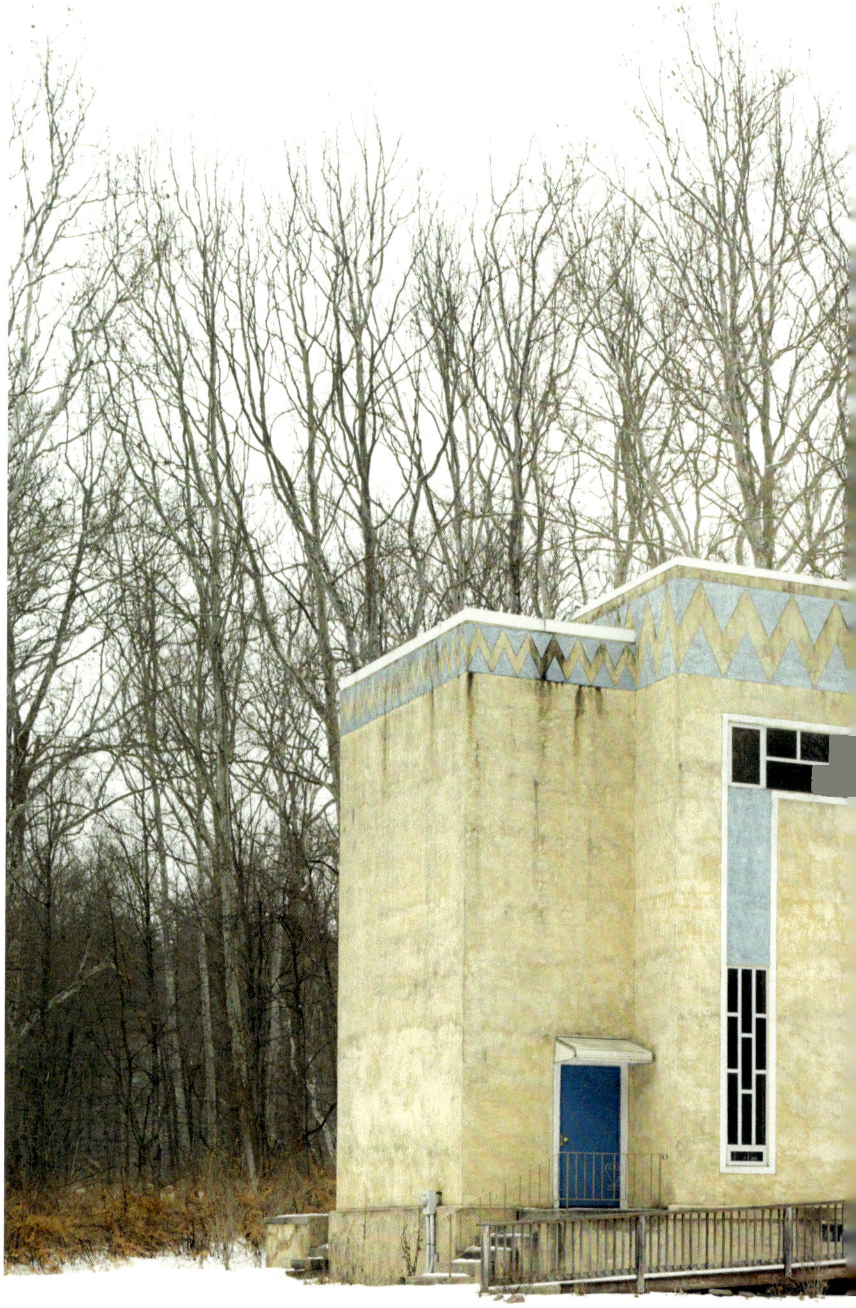

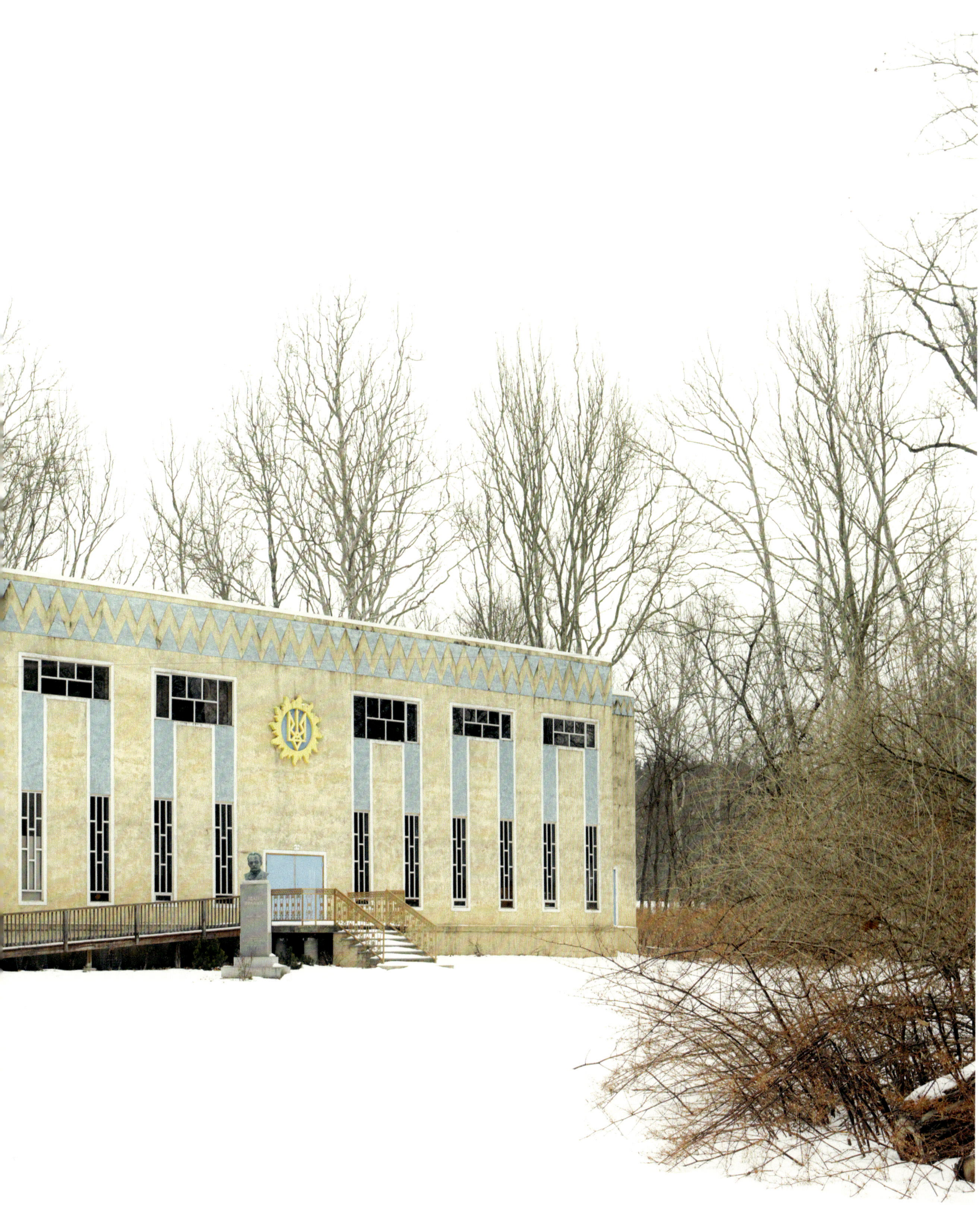

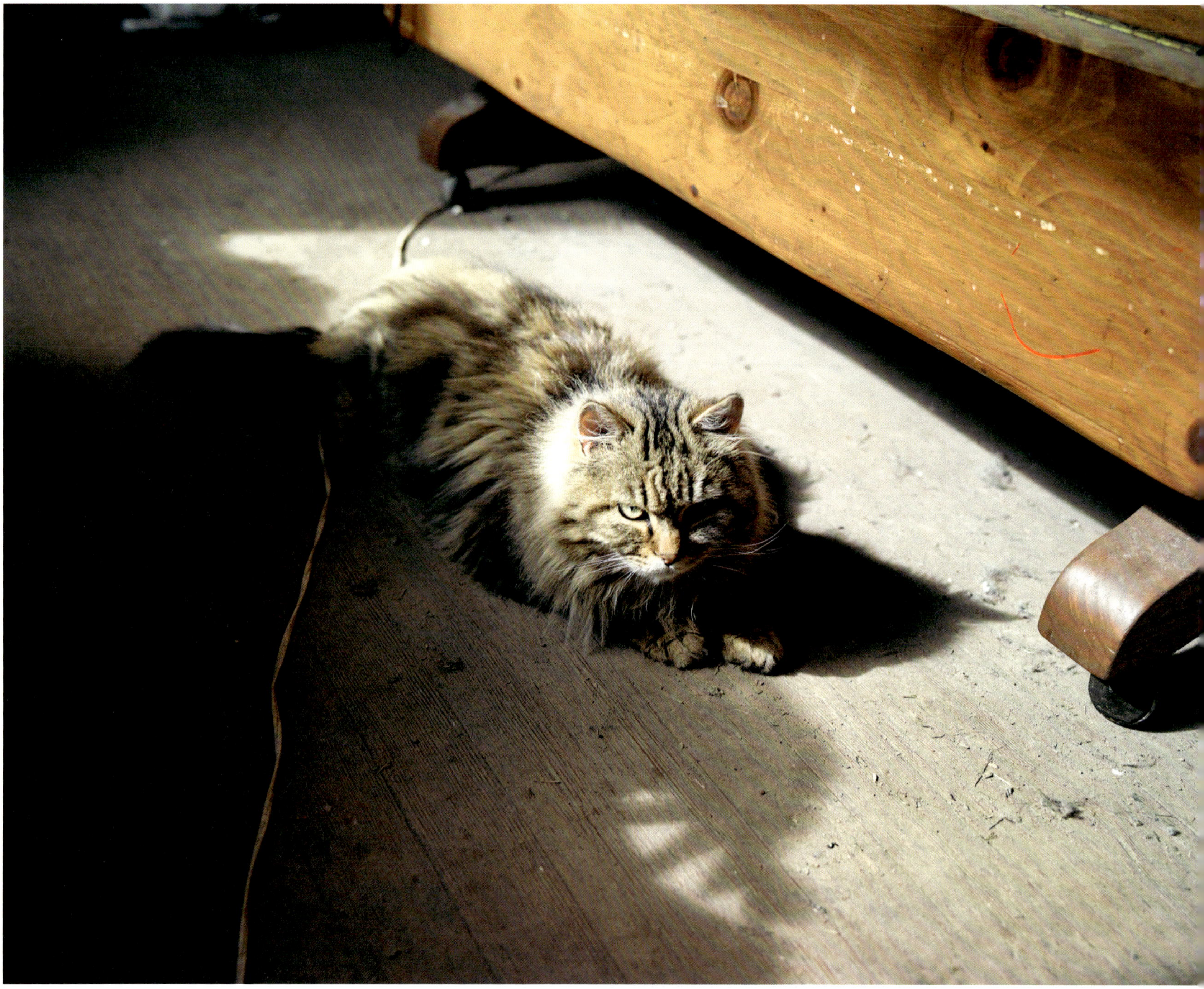

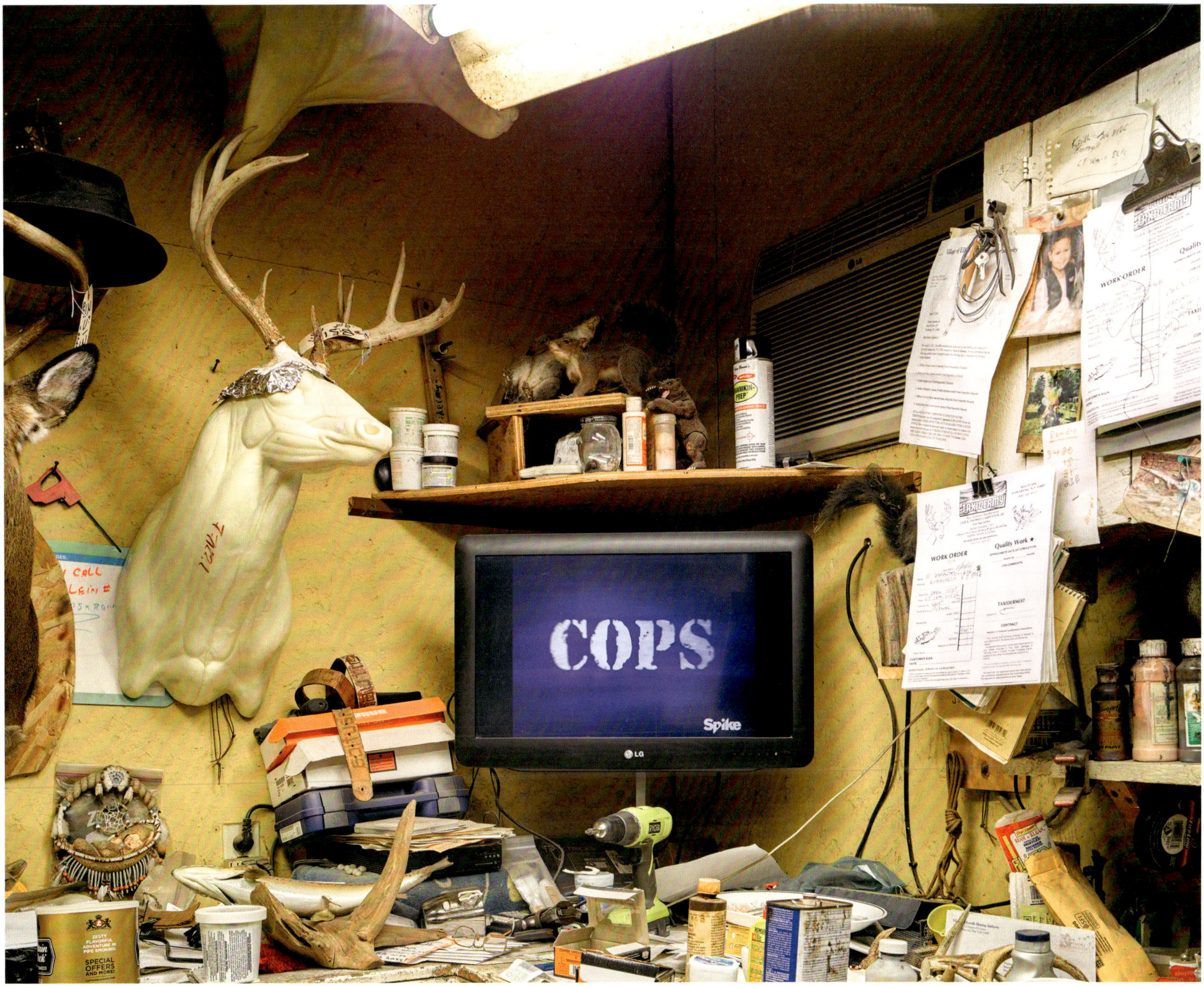
COPS
Spike
LG
WORK ORDER
Quality Work ★
TAXIDERMIST
TAXIDERMY

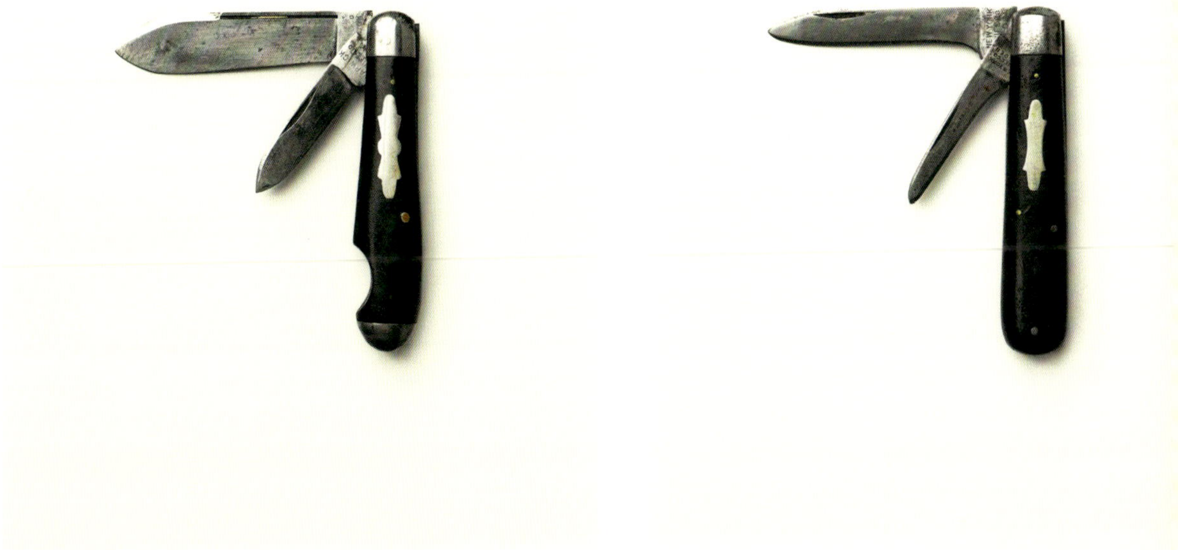

Easy Open Jack, Warwick Knife Co
c. 1911, Warwick, NY

Cigar Jack, New York Knife Co
c. 1923, Walden, NY

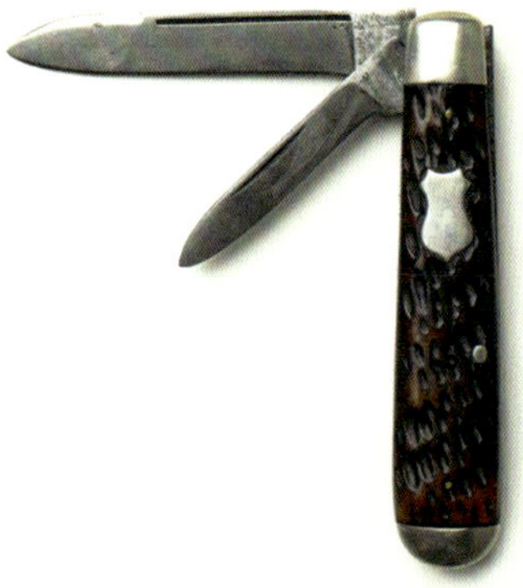

Brown Bone Jack, Electric Cutlery Co
c. 1915, Walden, NY

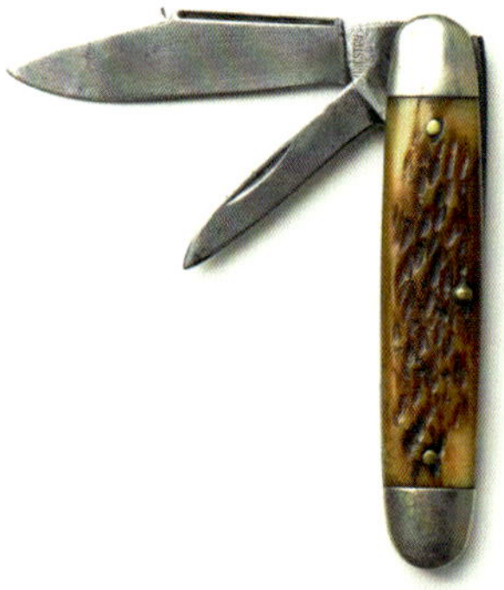

Imitation Bone Jack, Kingston Cutlery Co
c. 1944, Walden, NY

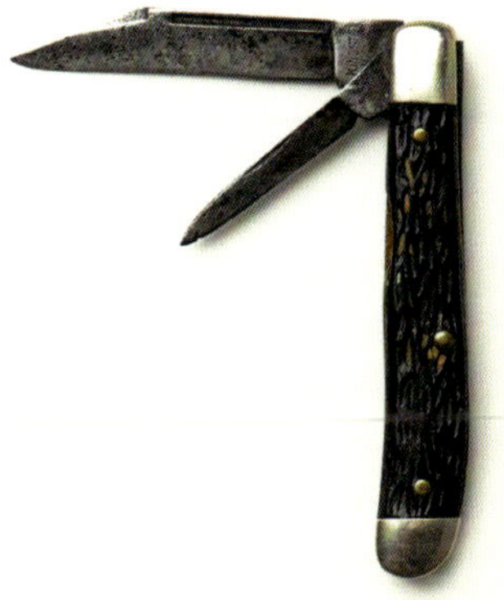

Imitation Bone Jack, Kingston Cutlery Co
c. 1946, Walden, NY

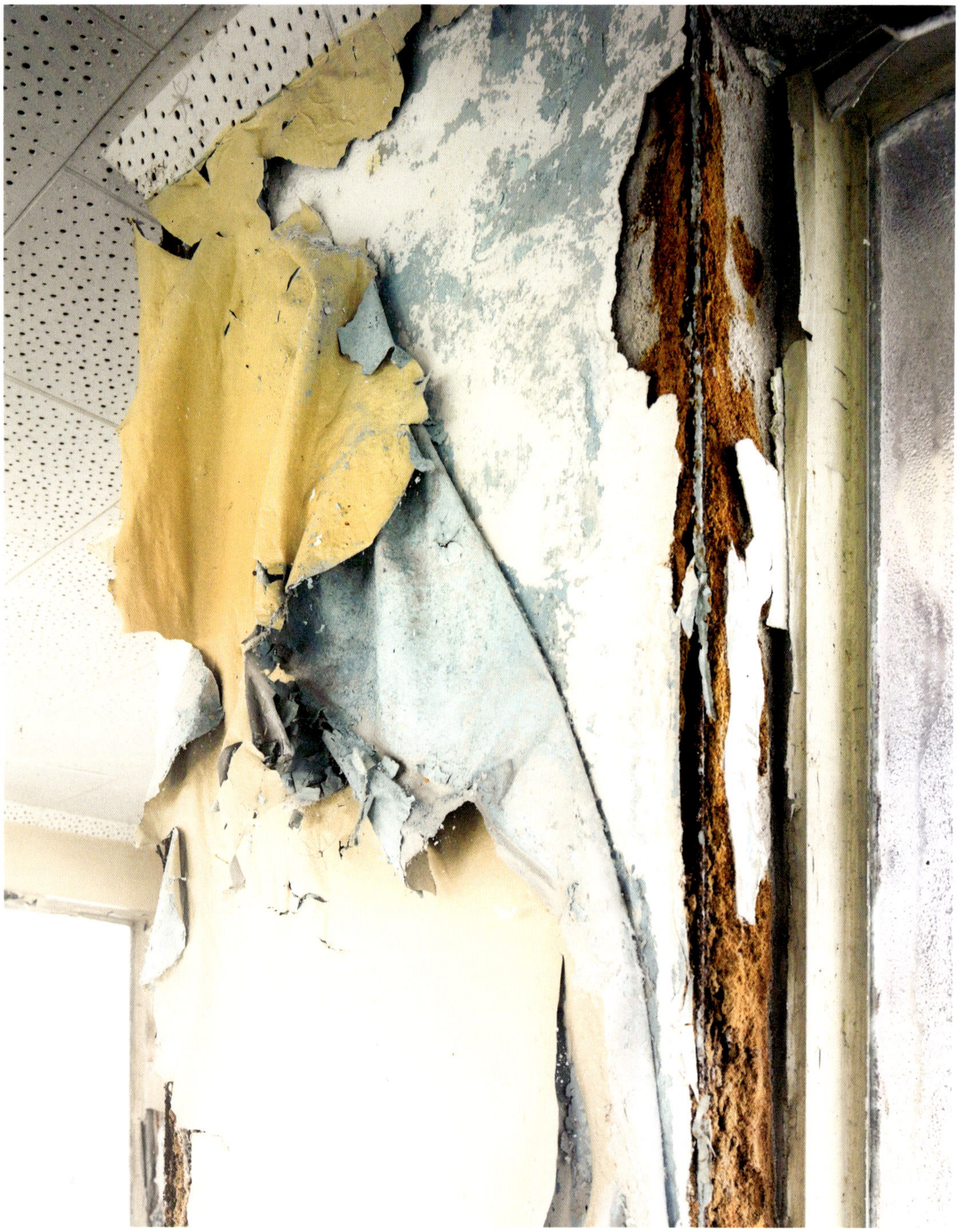

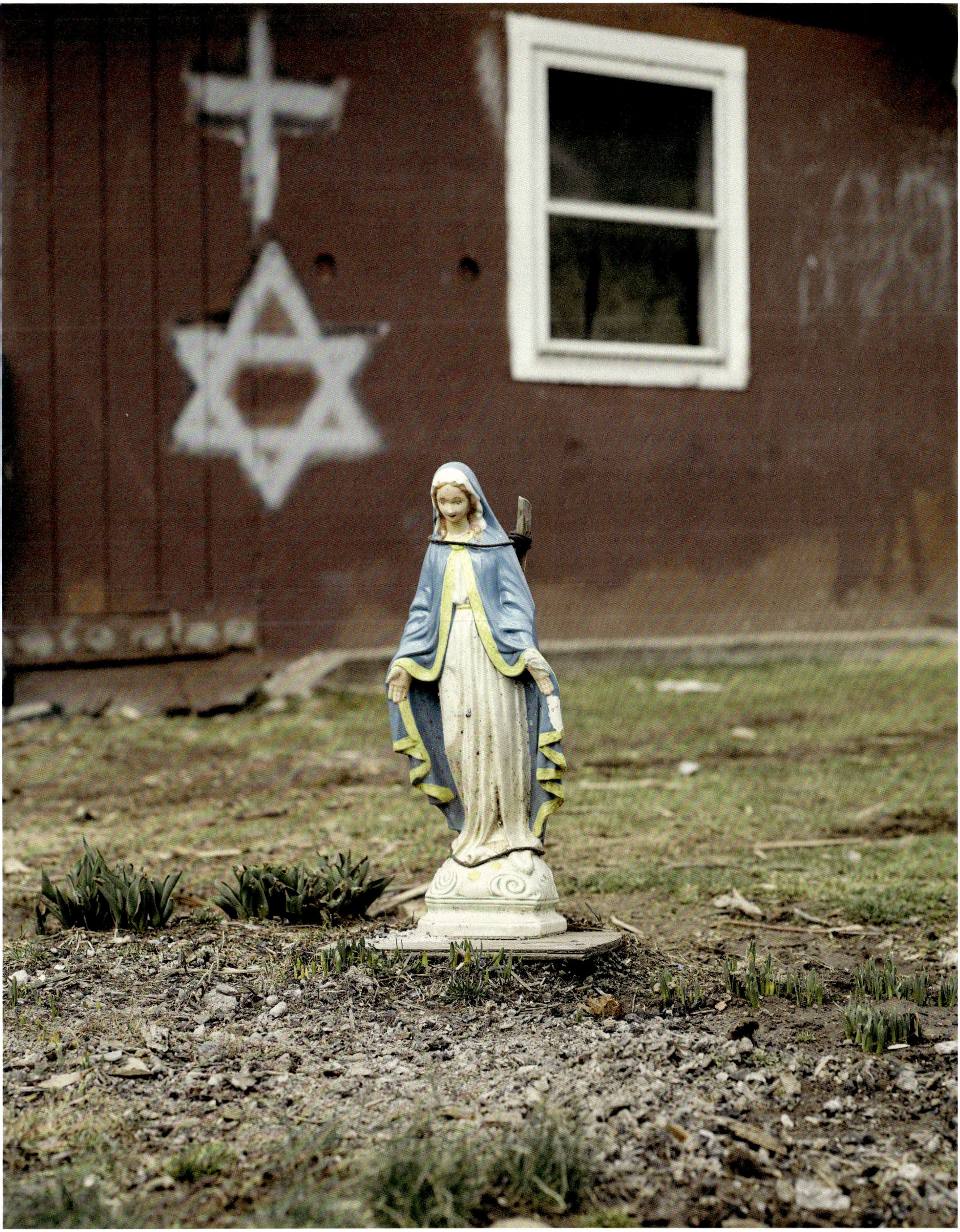

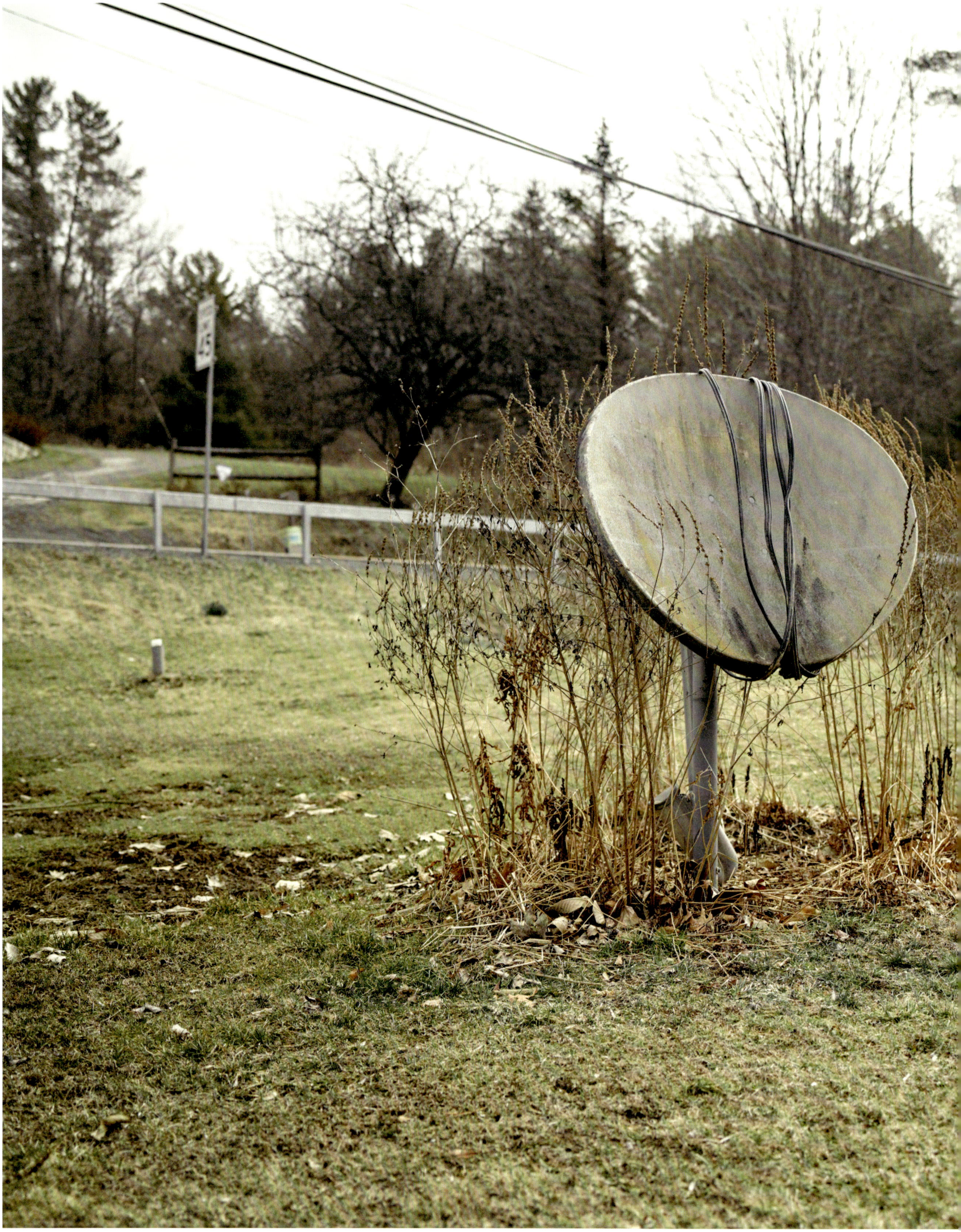

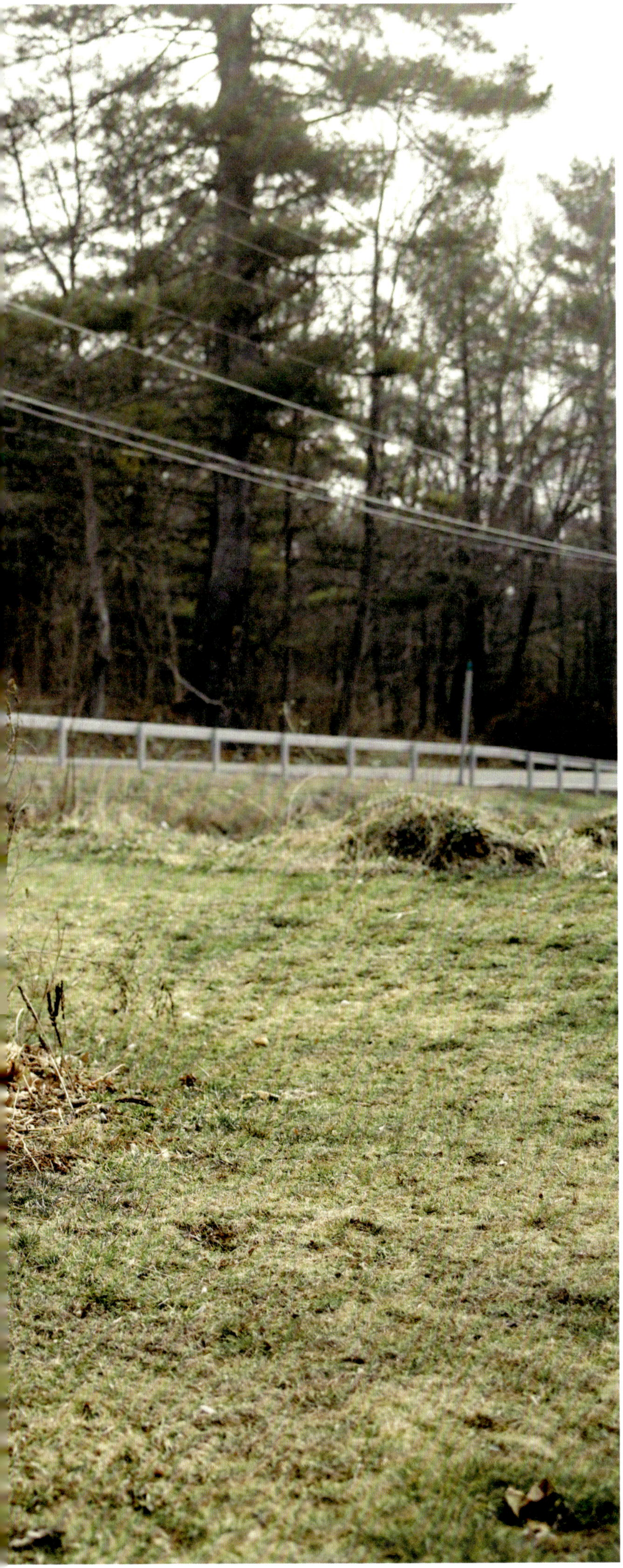

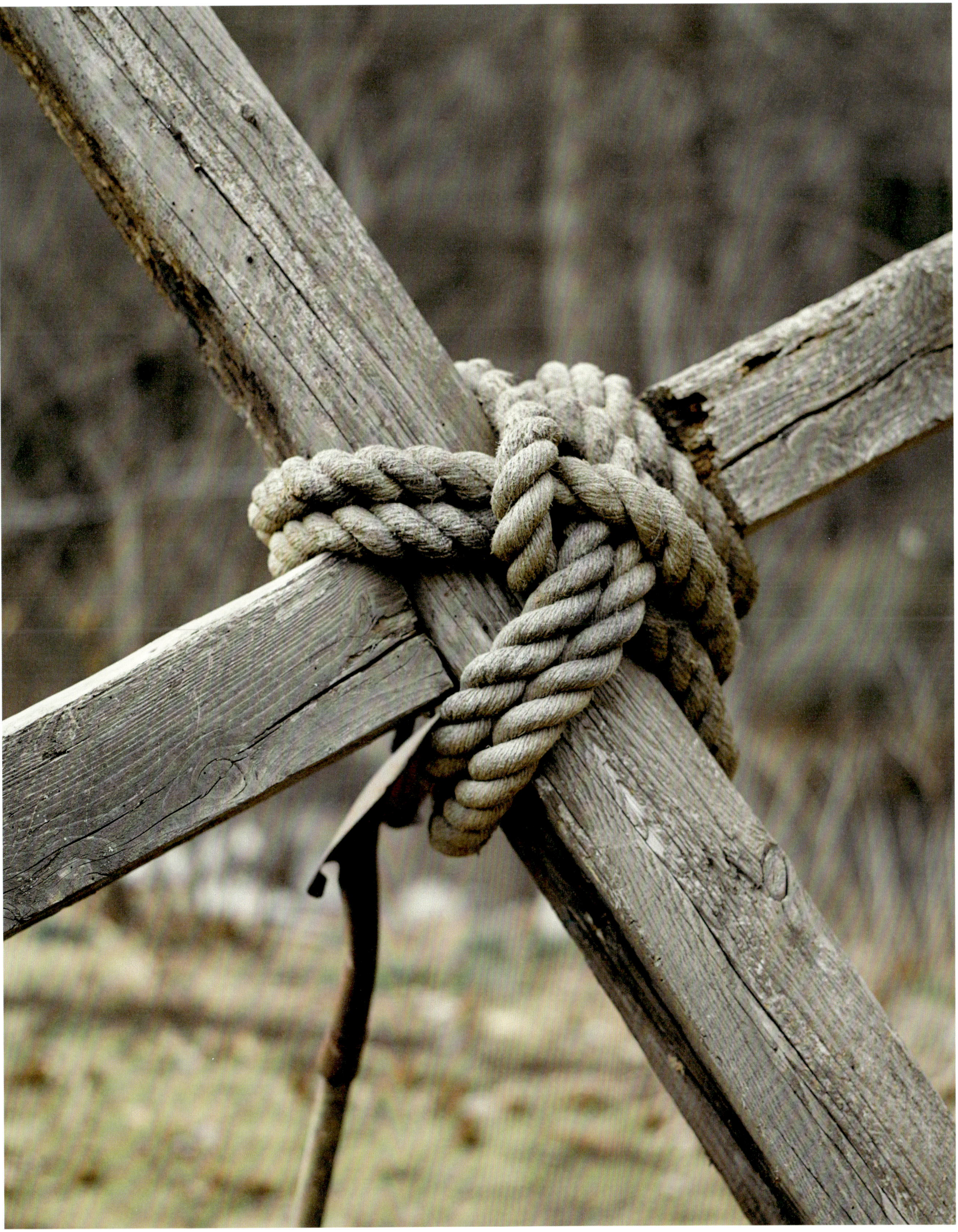

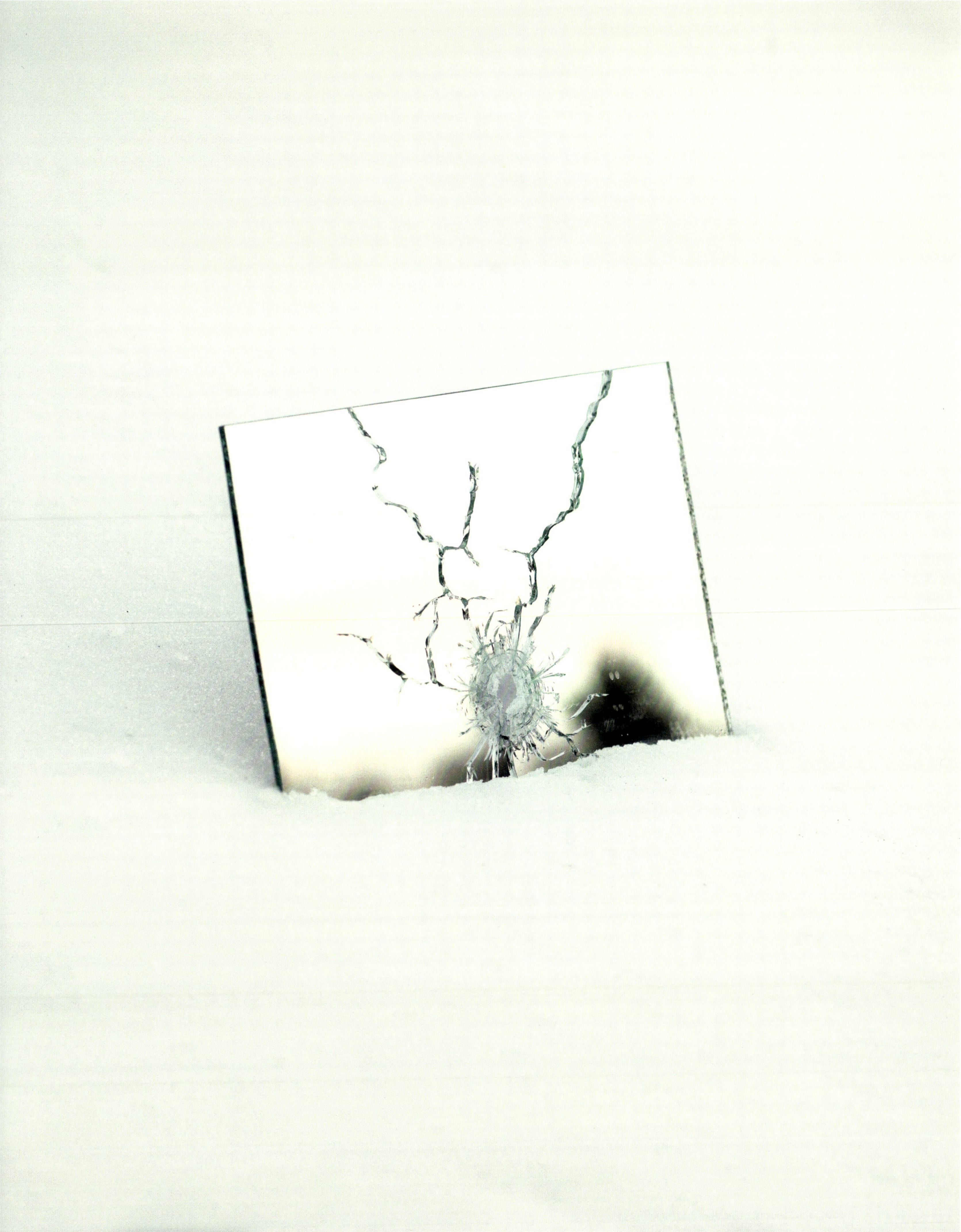

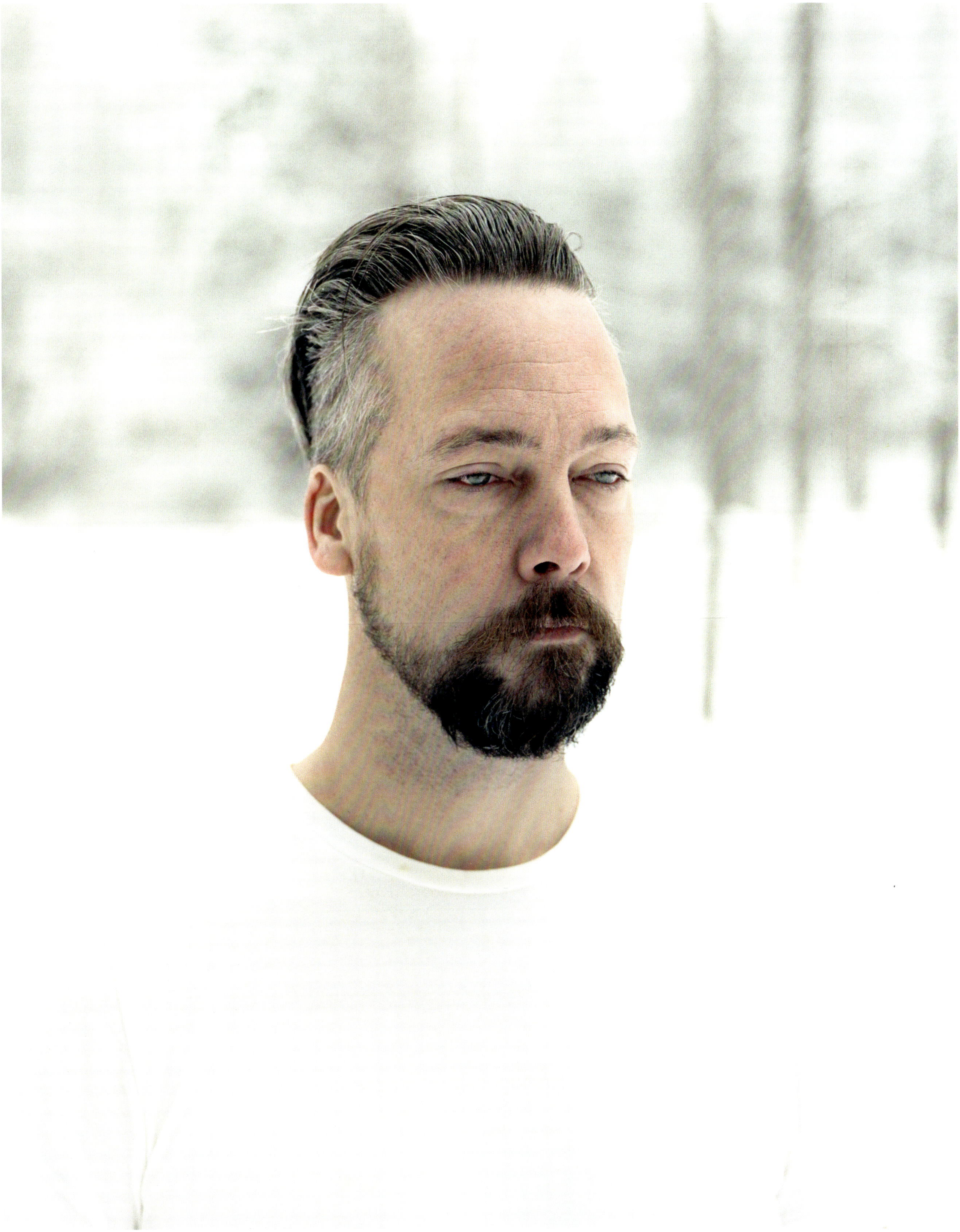

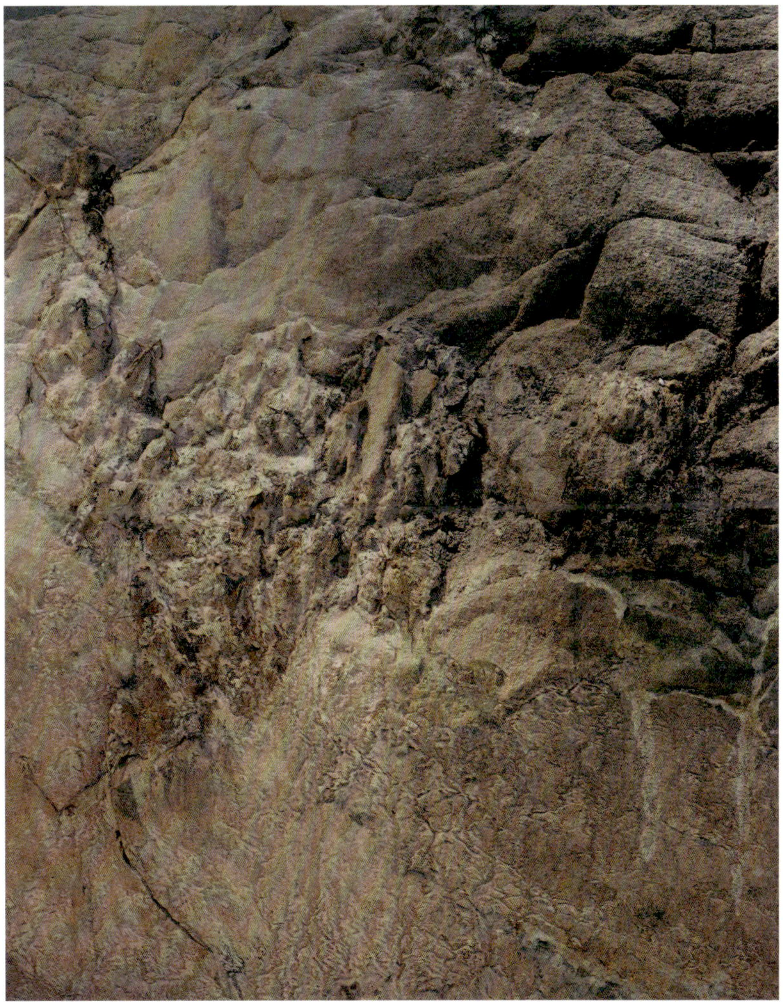

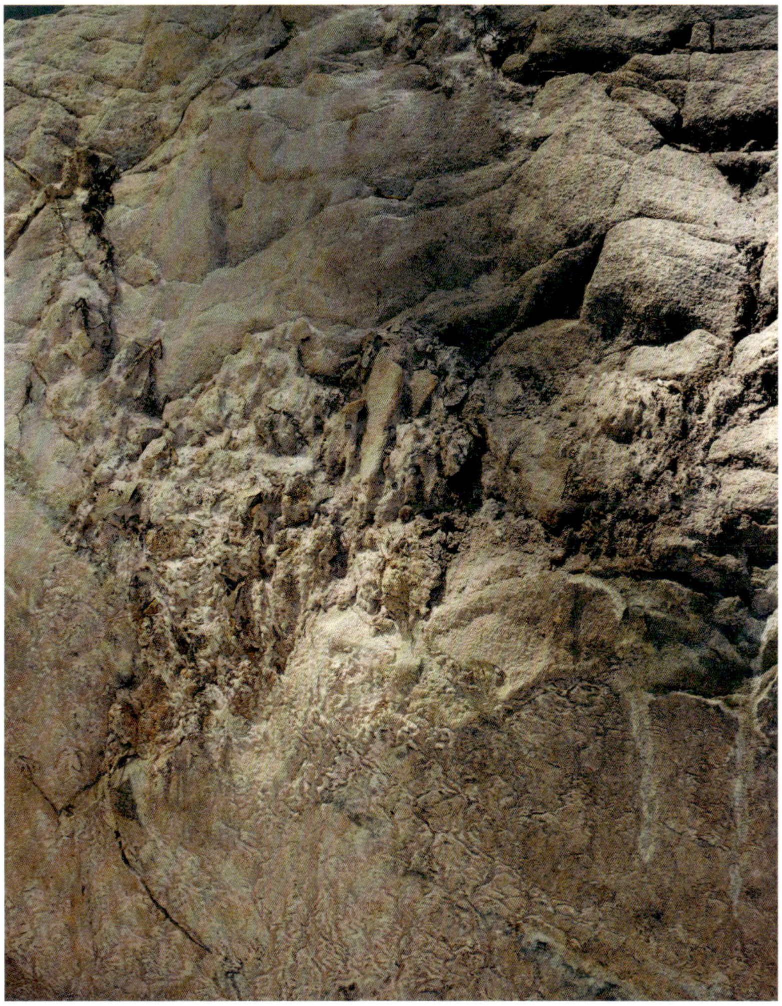

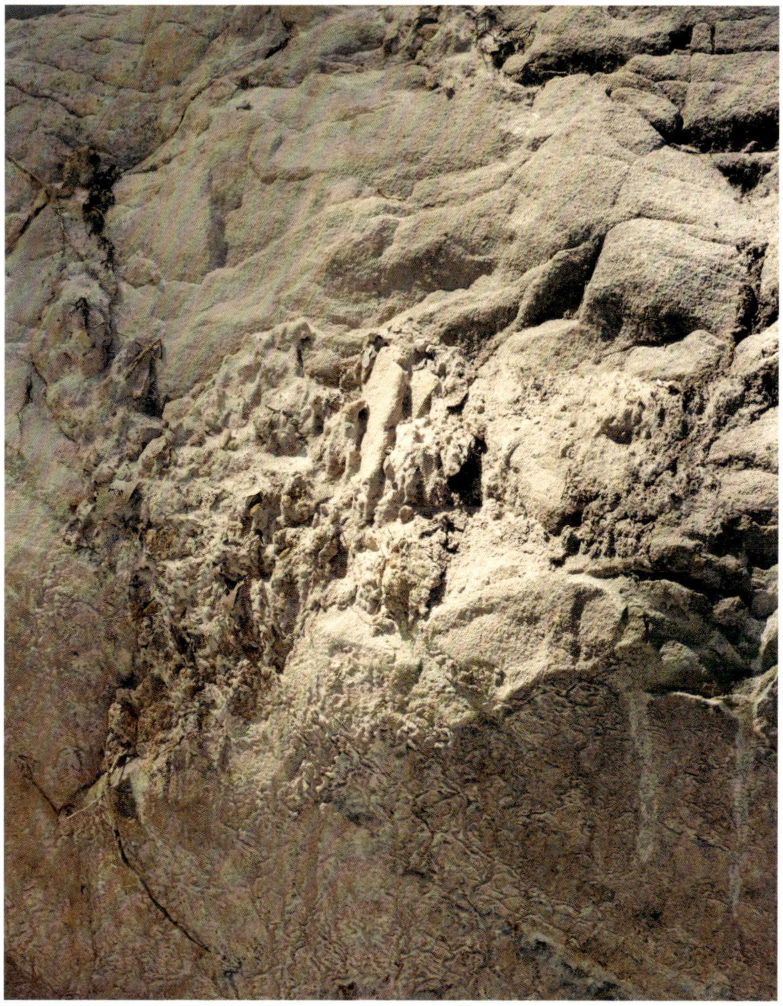

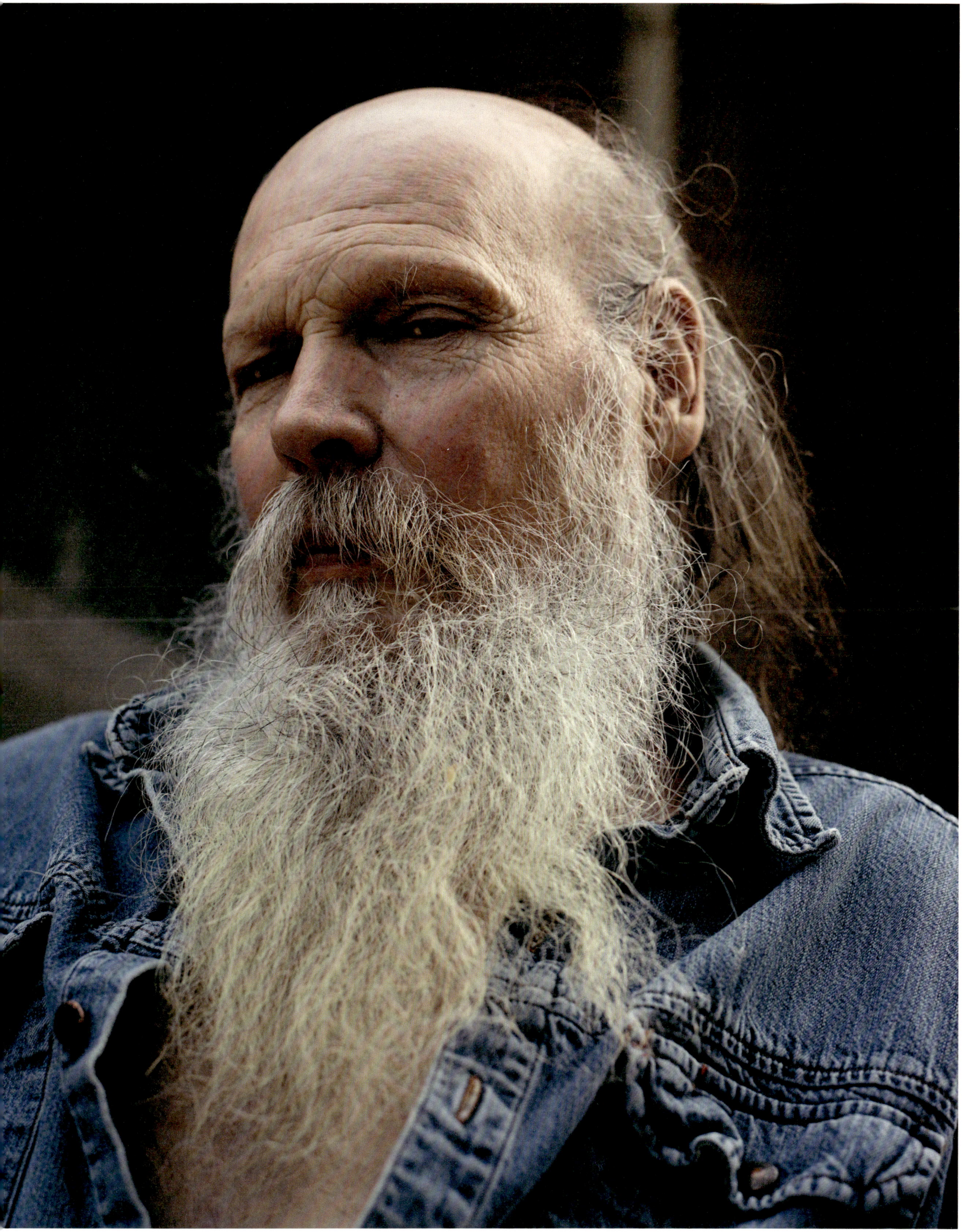

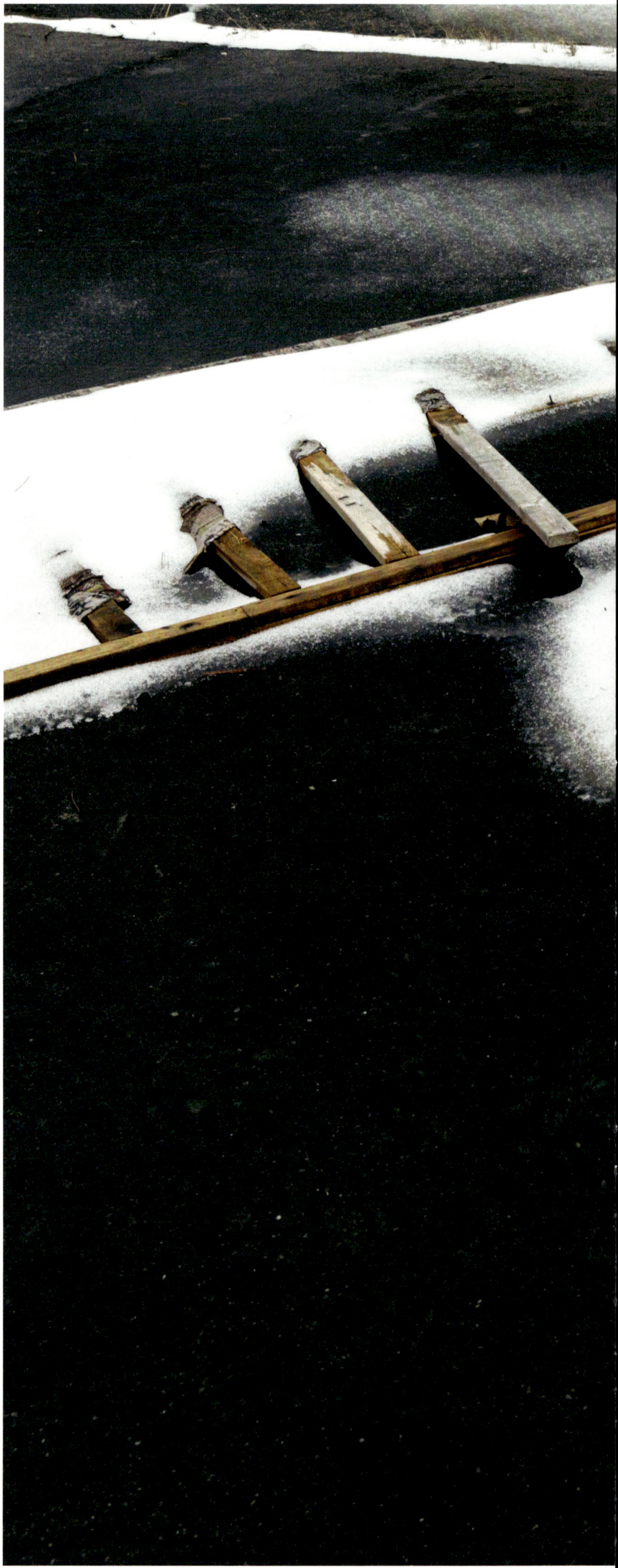

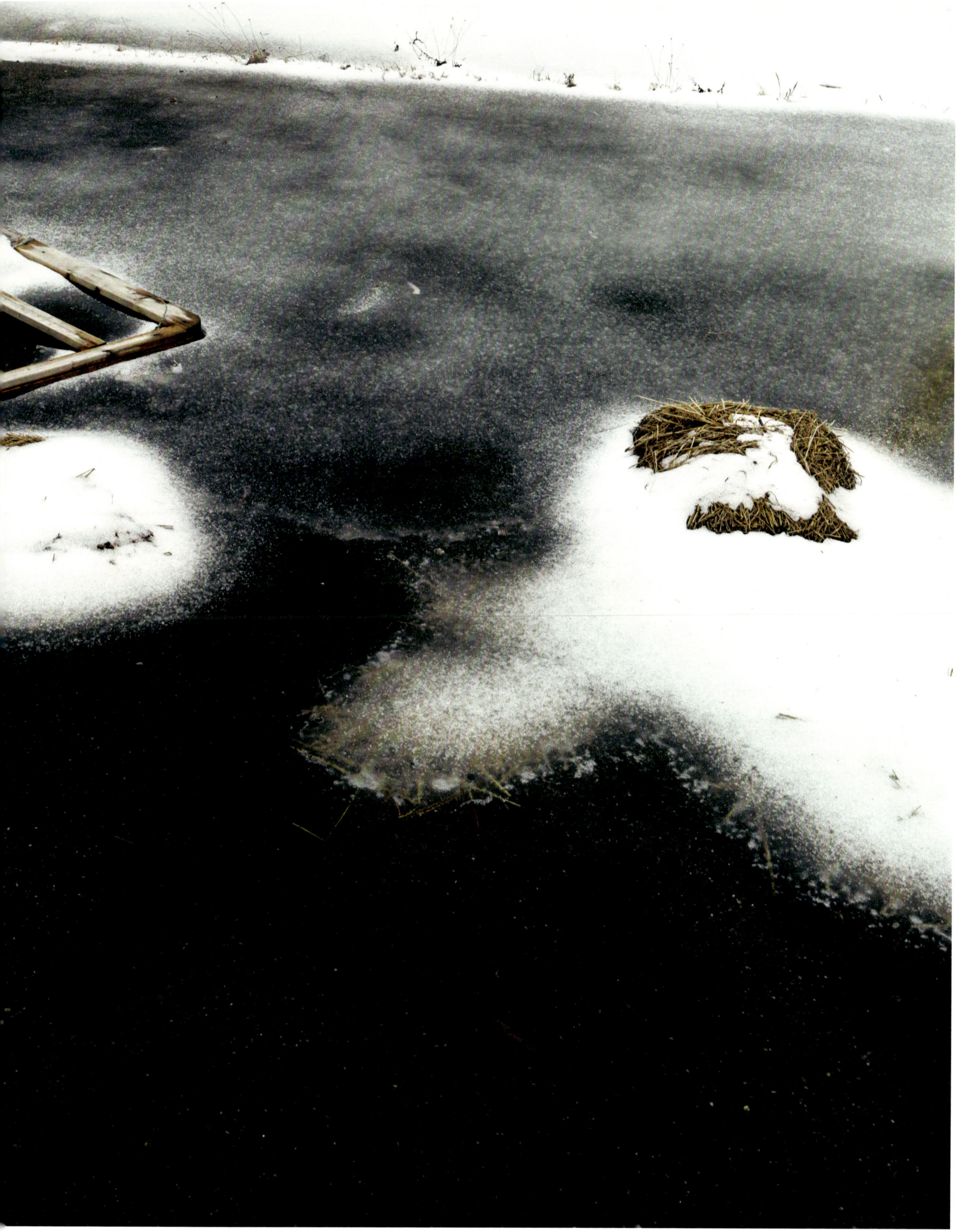

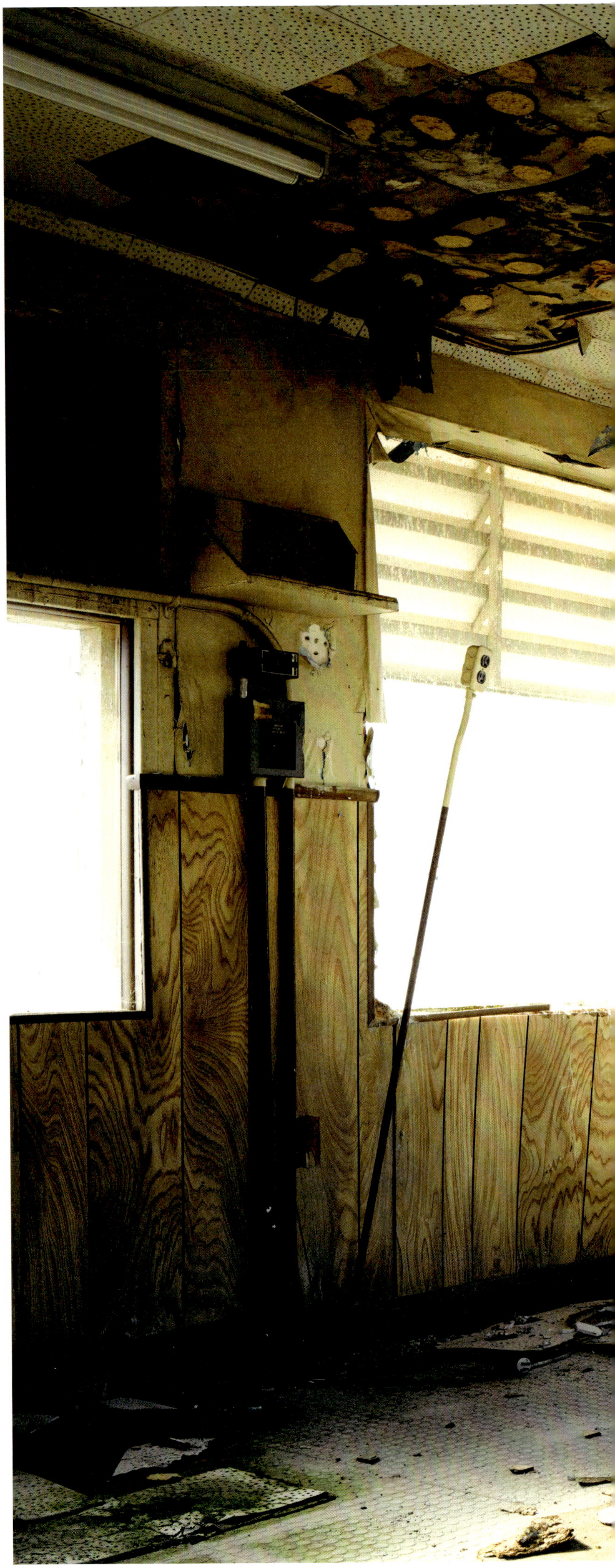

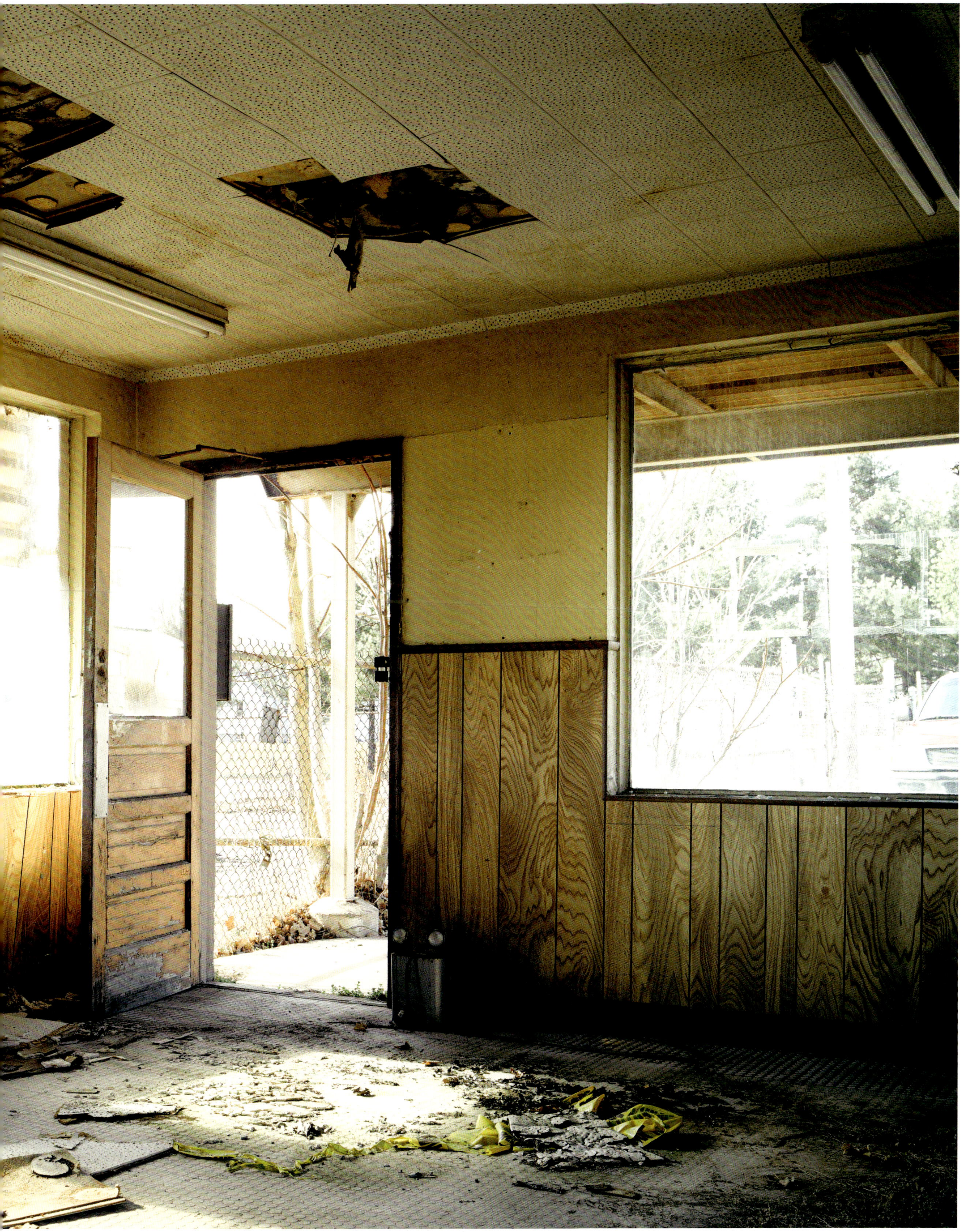

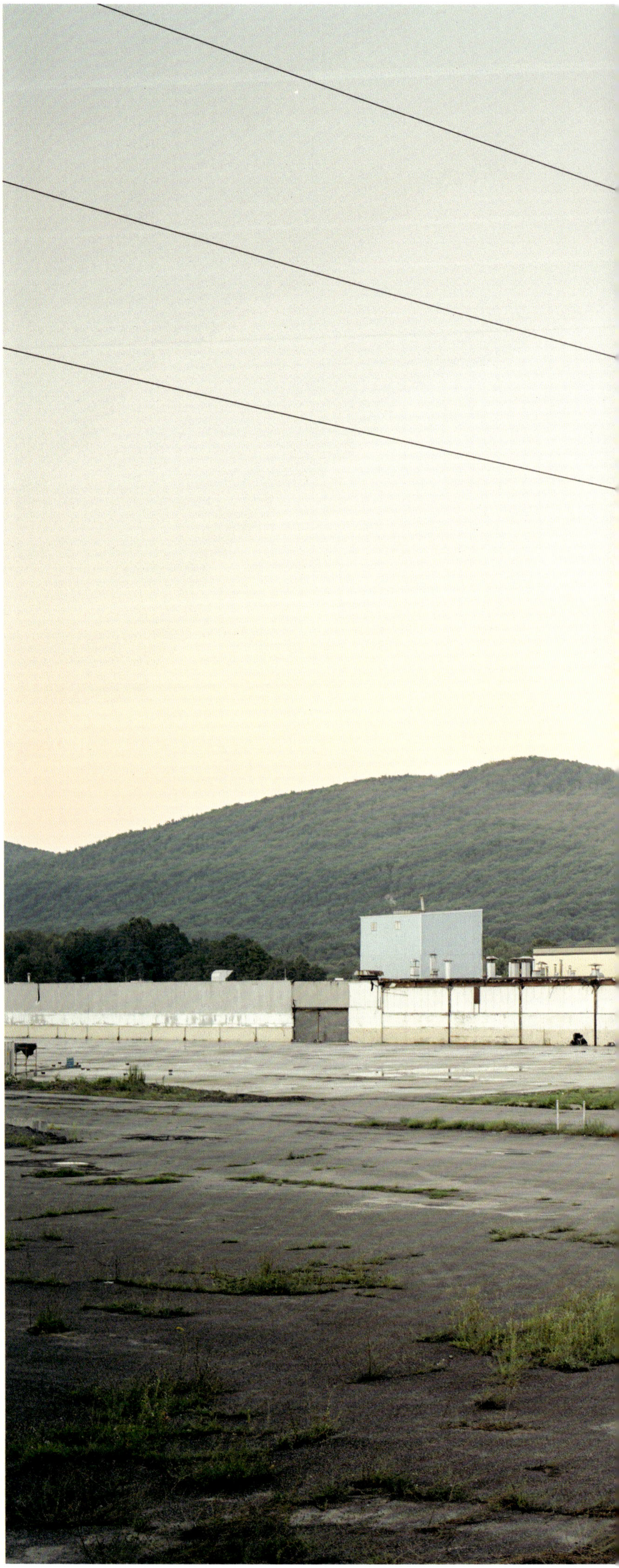

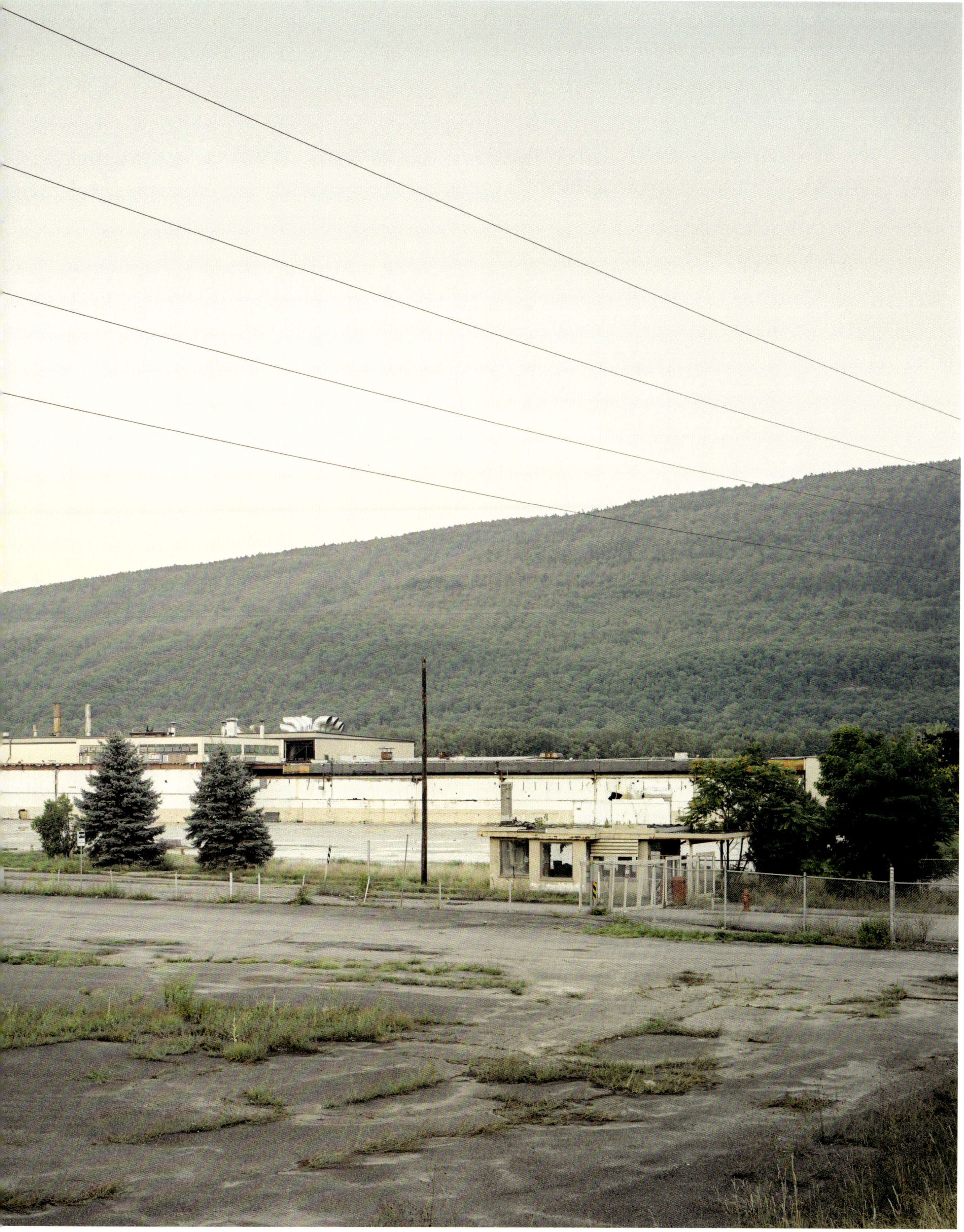

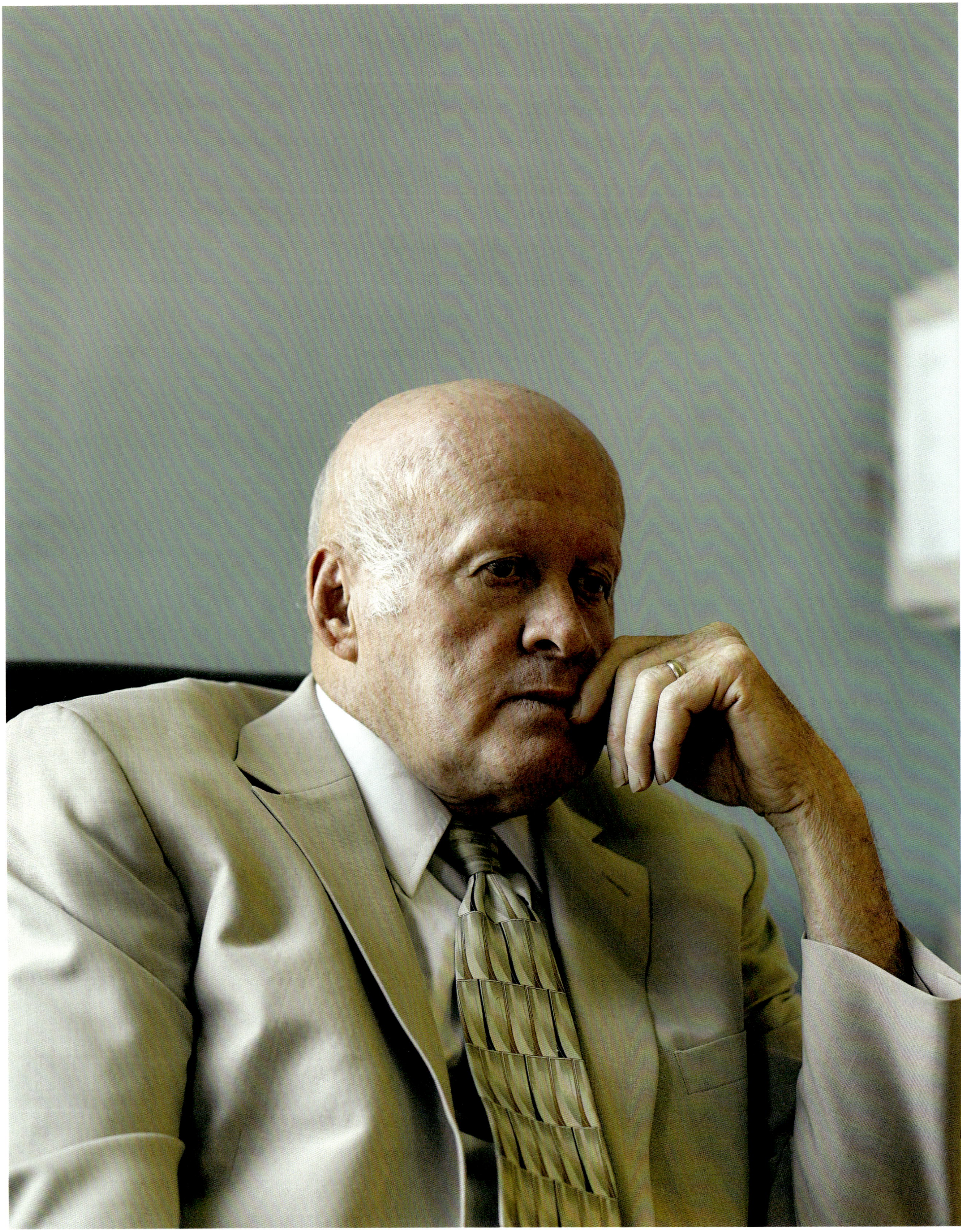

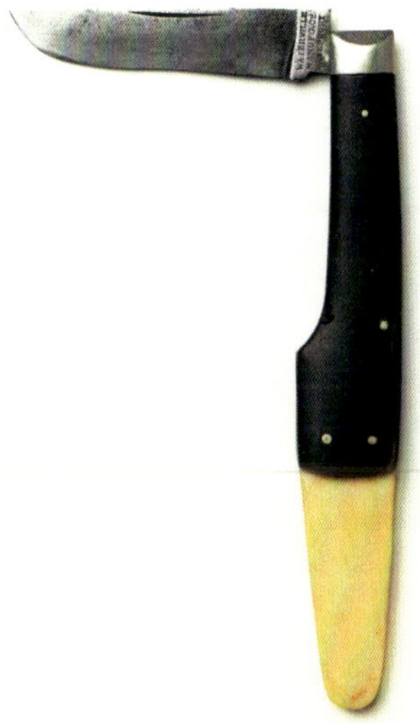

Budding Knife with Ivory Spud, Waterville Mfg Co
c. 1890, Waterbury, CT

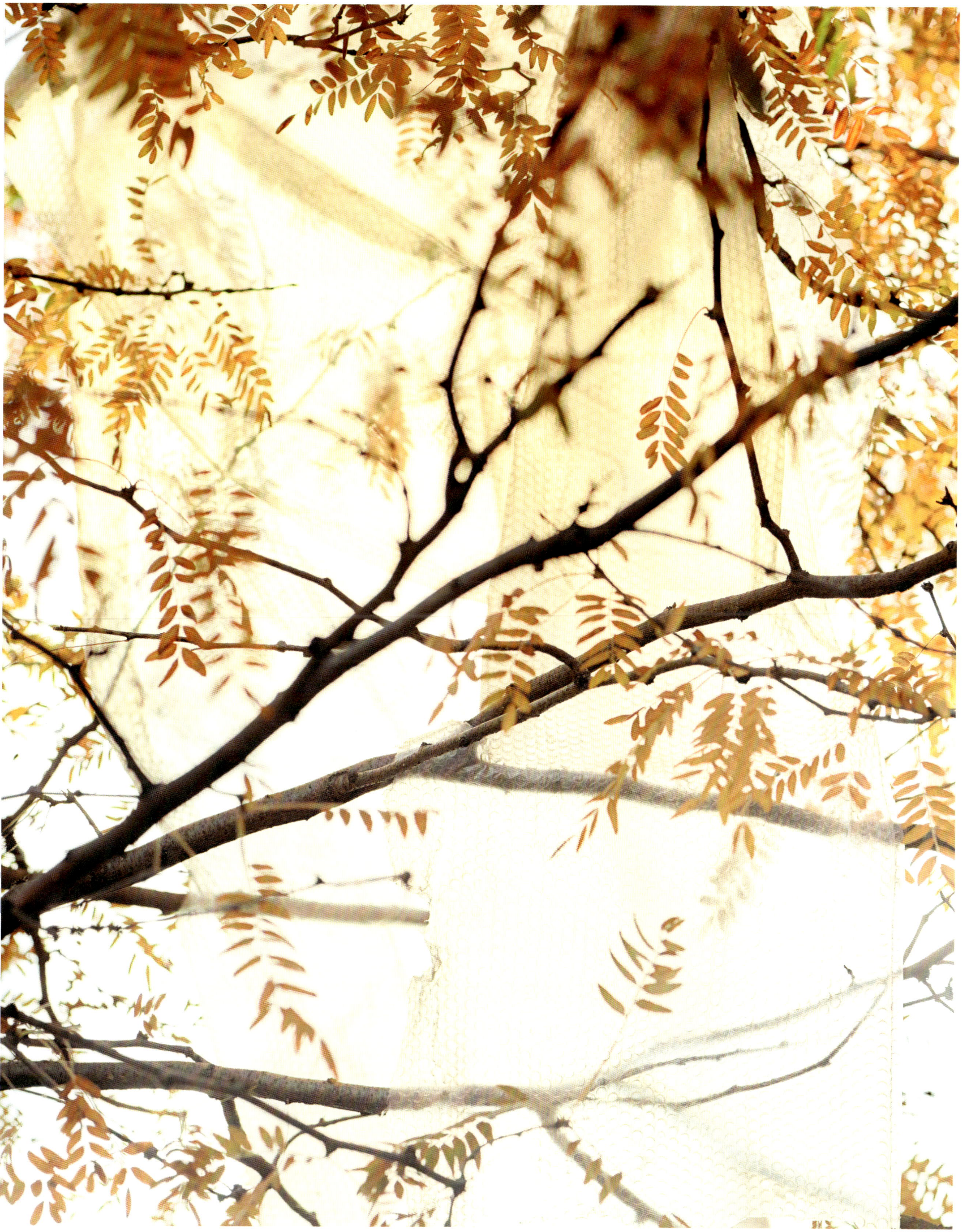

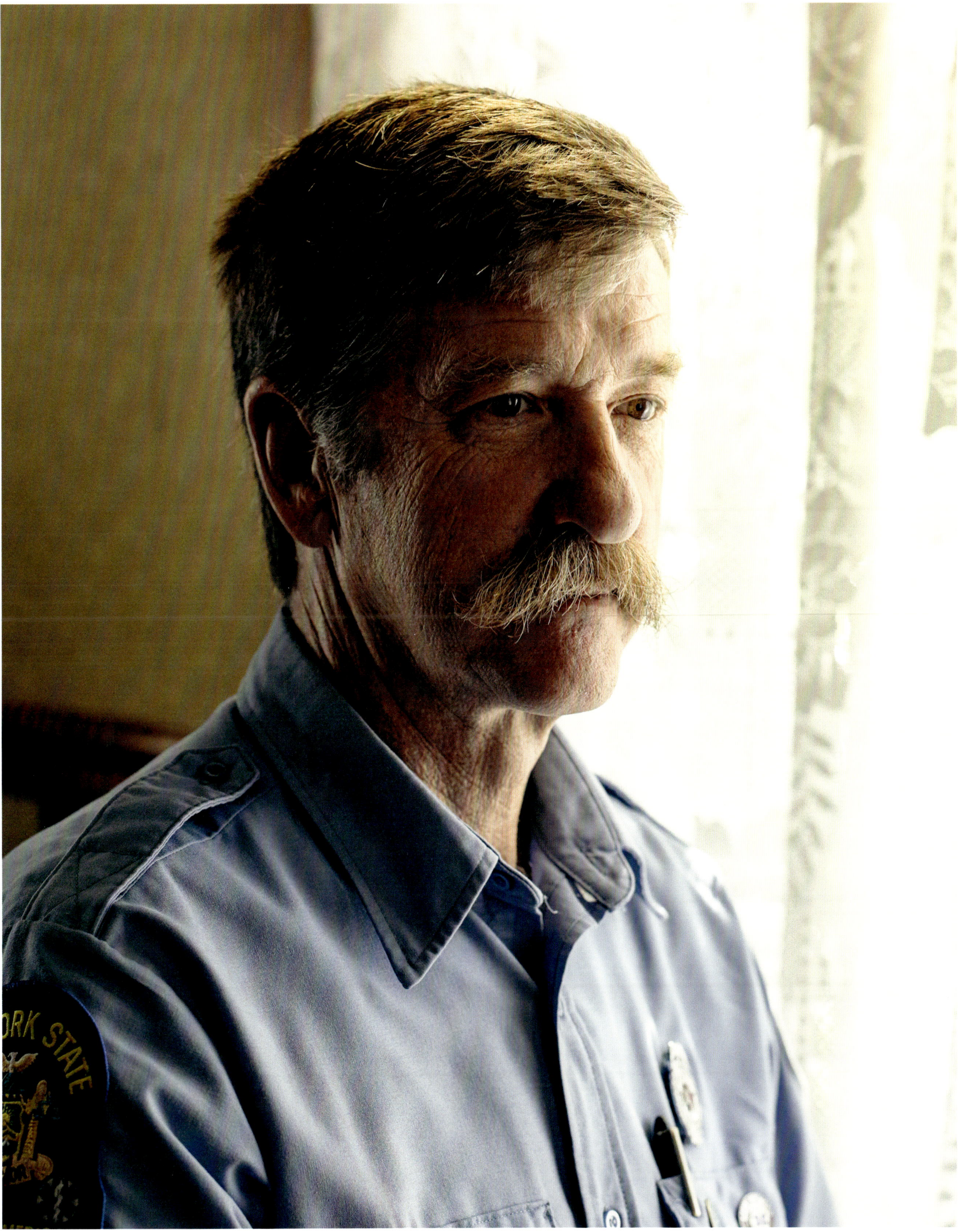

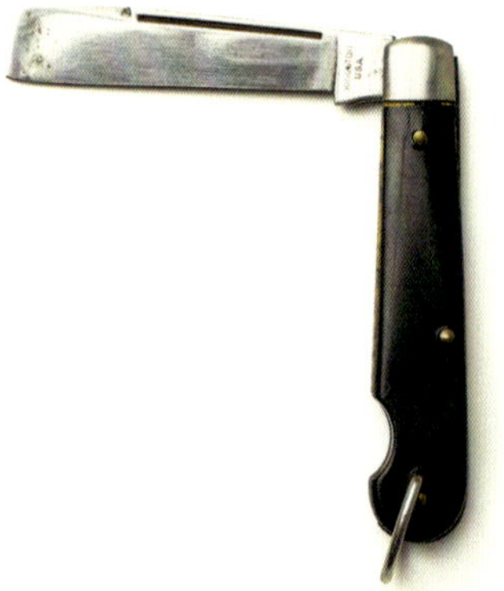

Rope Knife, Kingston Cutlery Co
c. 1948, Walden, NY

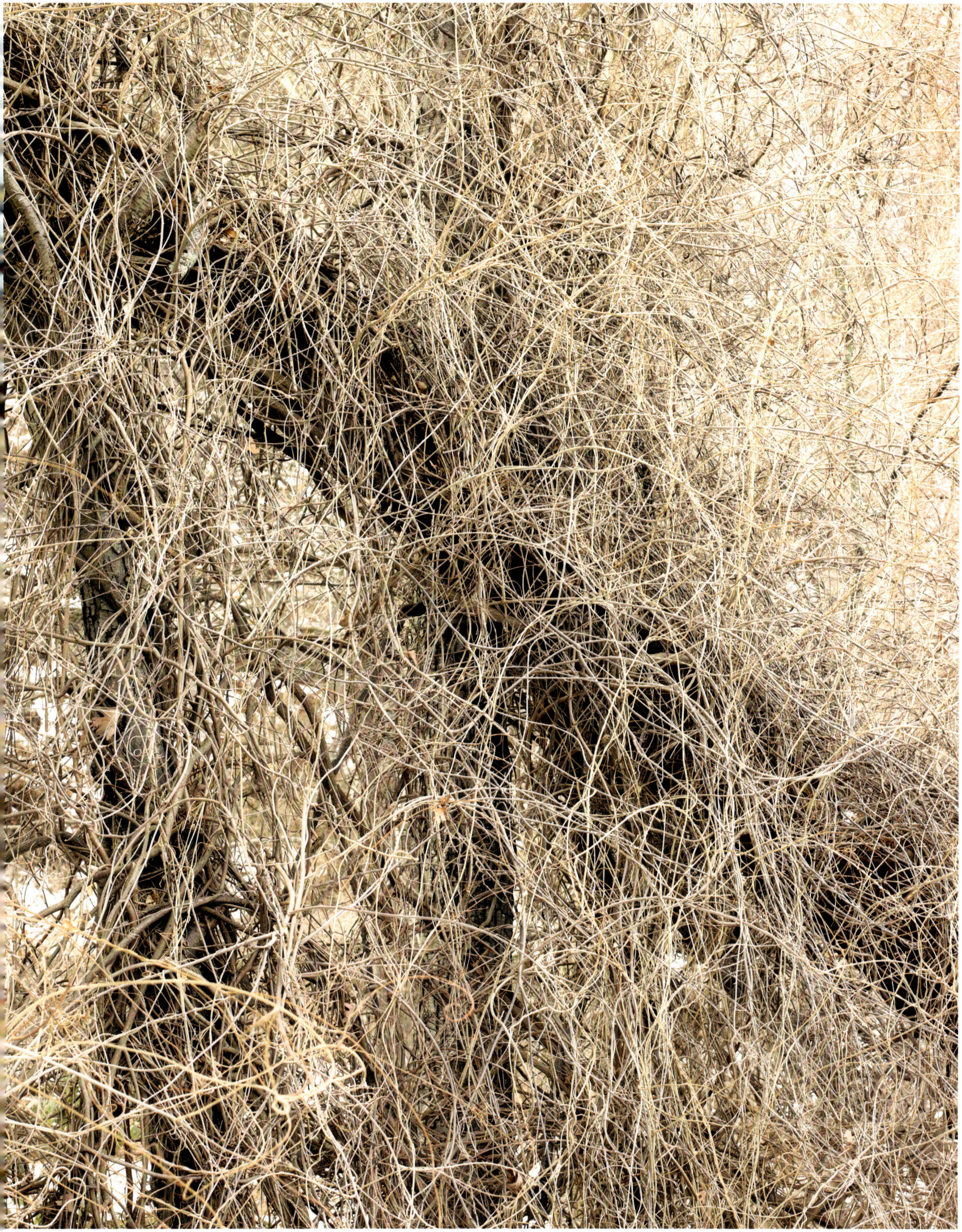

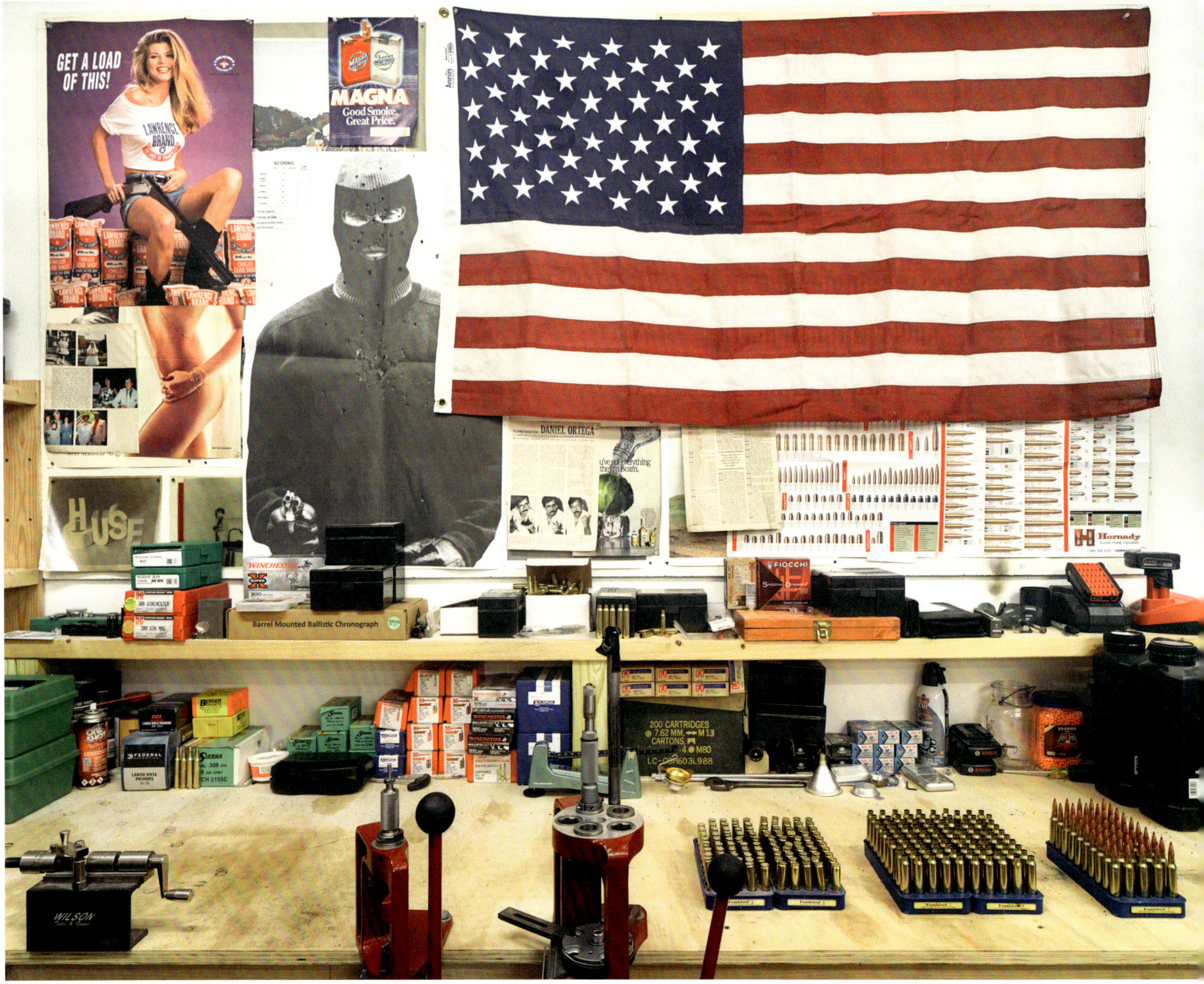
GET A LOAD OF THIS!
LAWRENCE BRAND
MAGNA
Good Smoke, Great Price.
DANIEL ORTEGA
Barrel Mounted Ballistic Chronograph
WINCHESTER
FIOCCHI
200 CARTRIDGES
7.62 MM M13
CARTONS, 4 M80
Hornady
WILSON

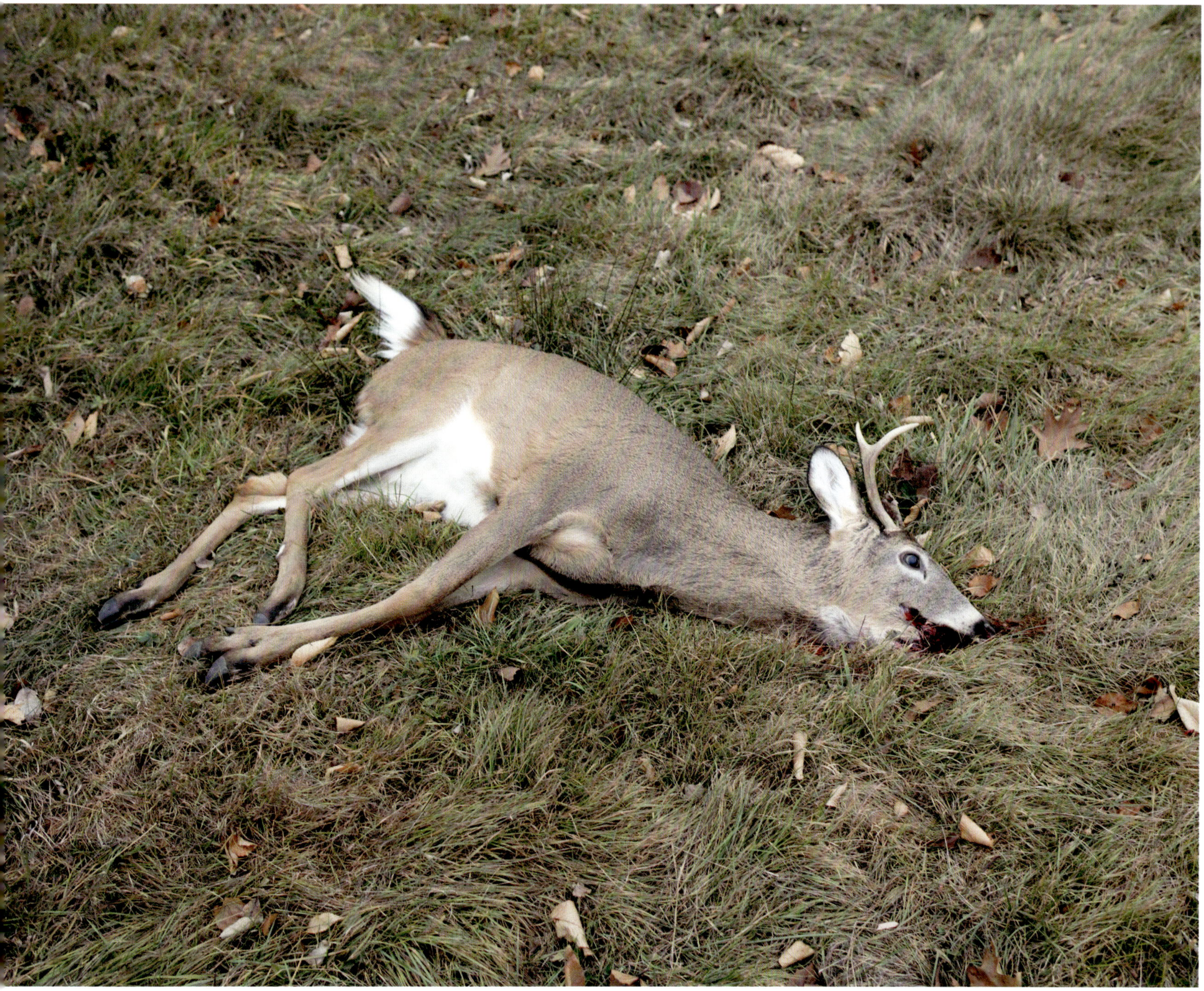

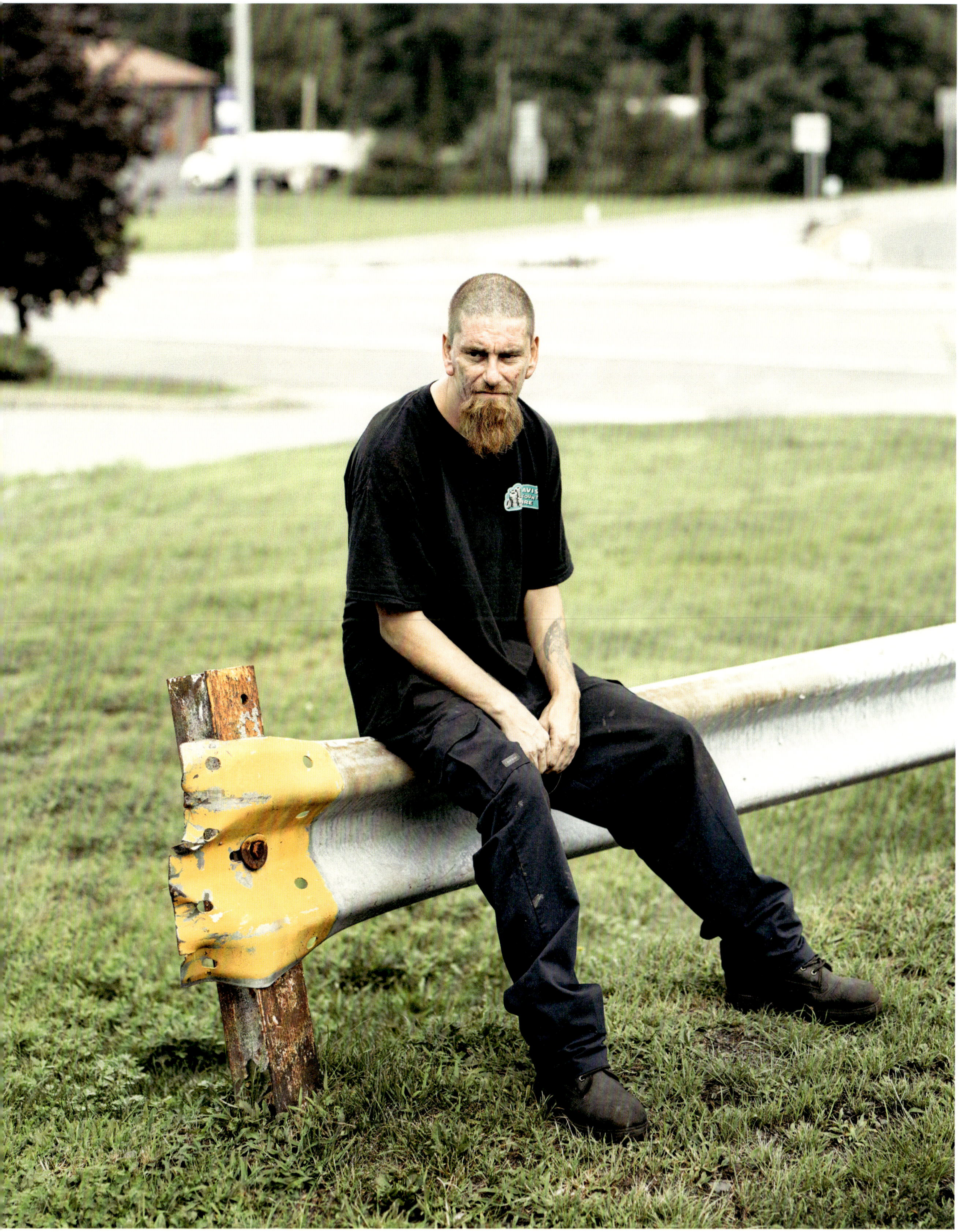

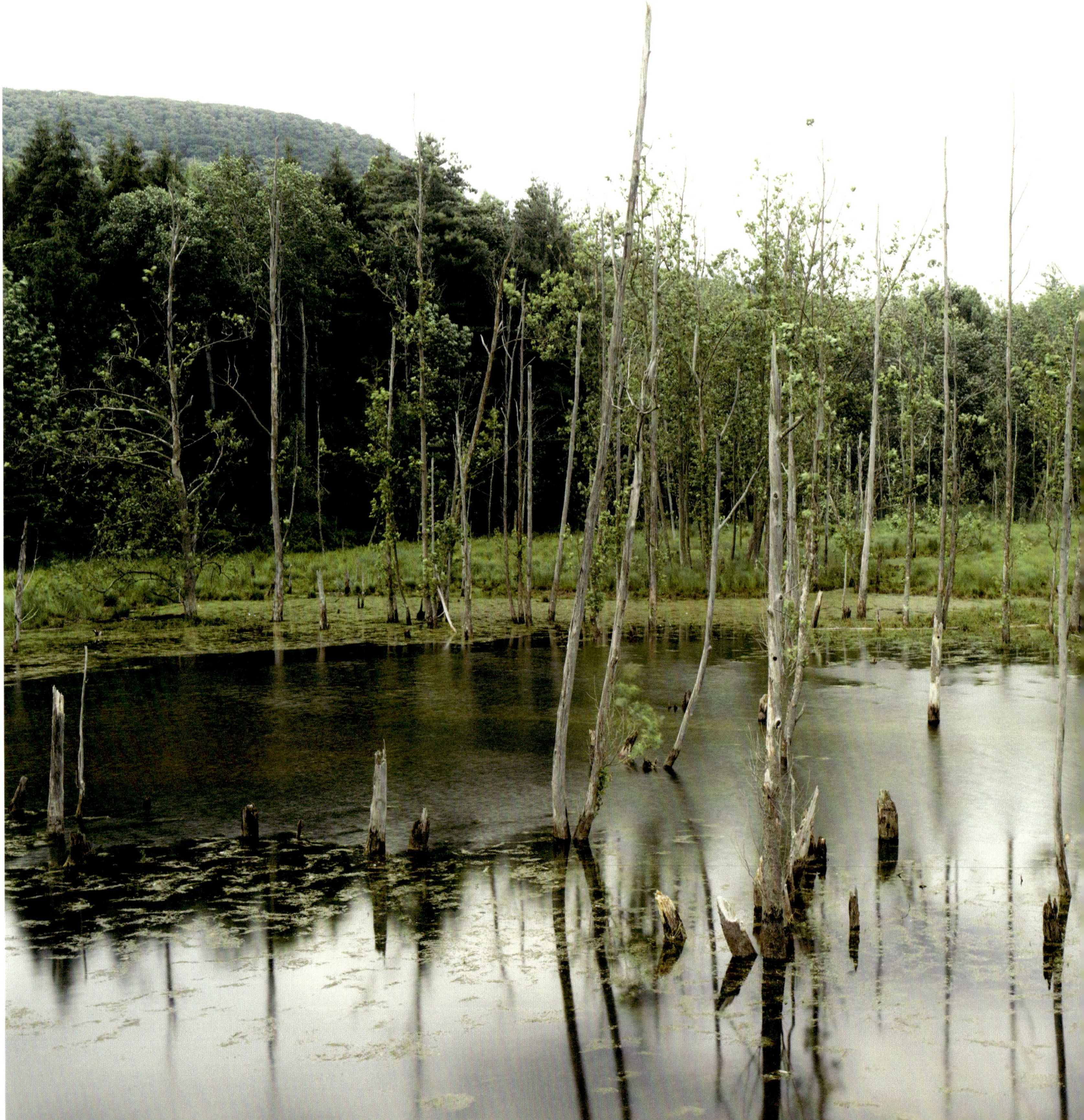

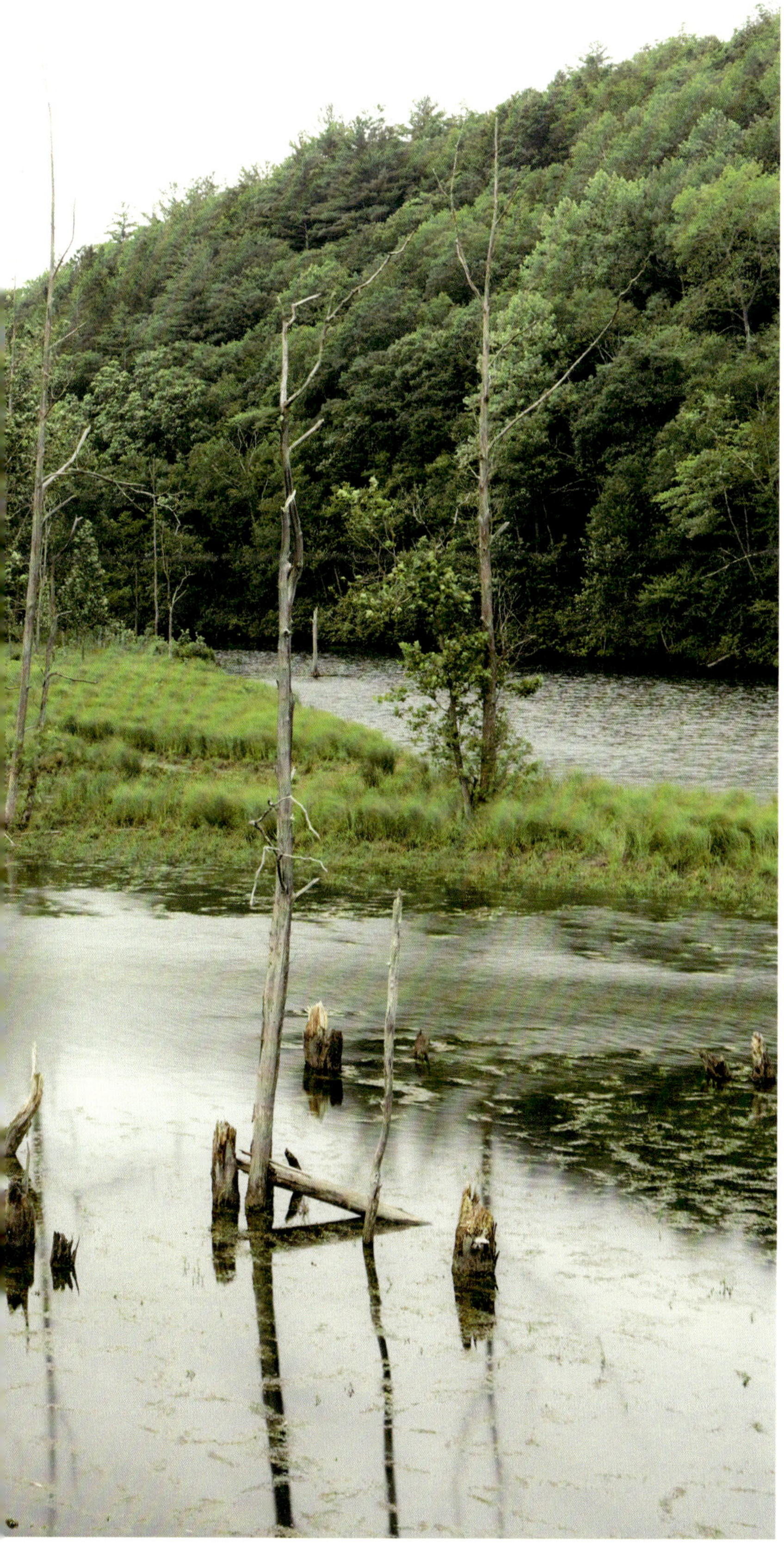

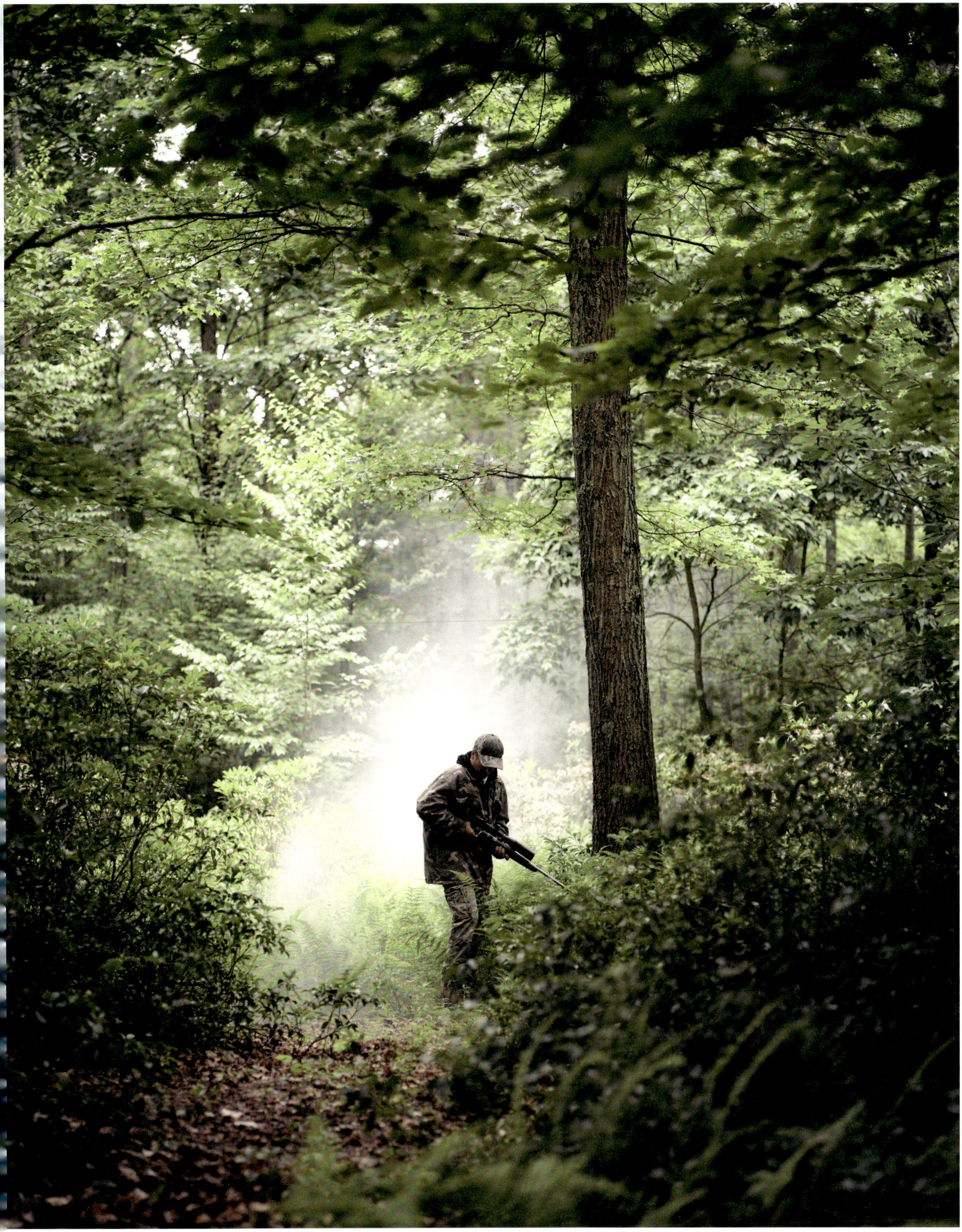

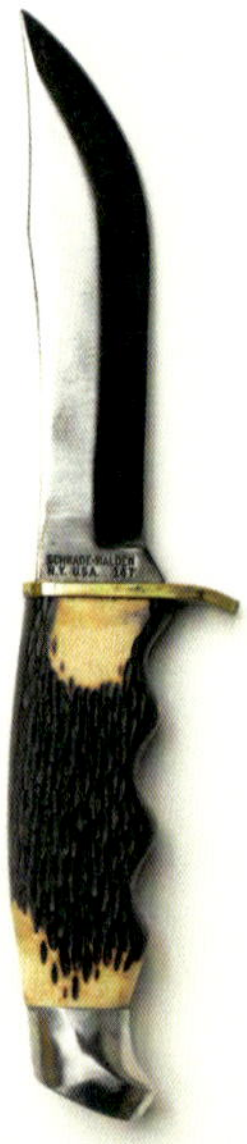

147 Fixed Blade, Schrade-Walden
c. 1963, Wawarsing, NY

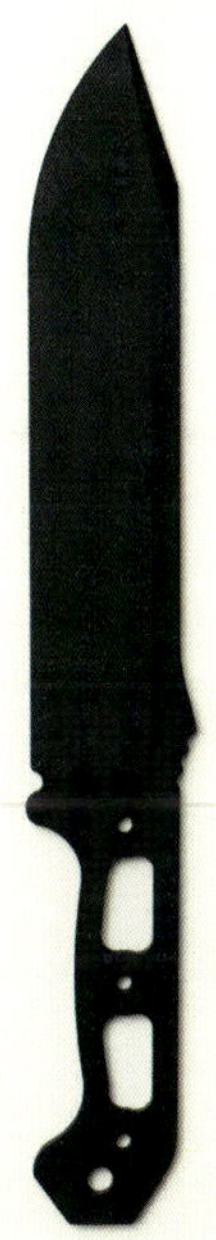

BK&T Combat Bowie (blank), Camillus Cutlery Co
c. 1972, Camillus, NY

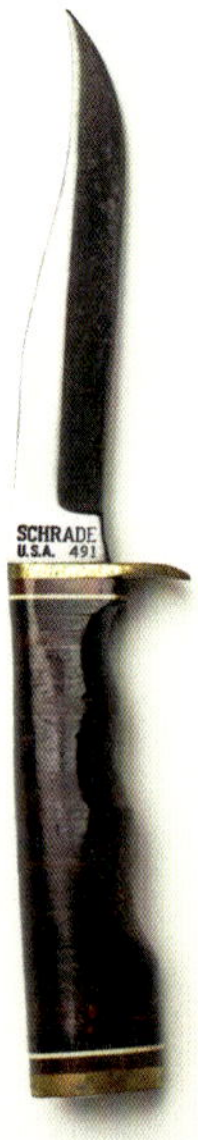

491 Fixed Blade, Schrade-Walden
1973, Wawarsing, NY

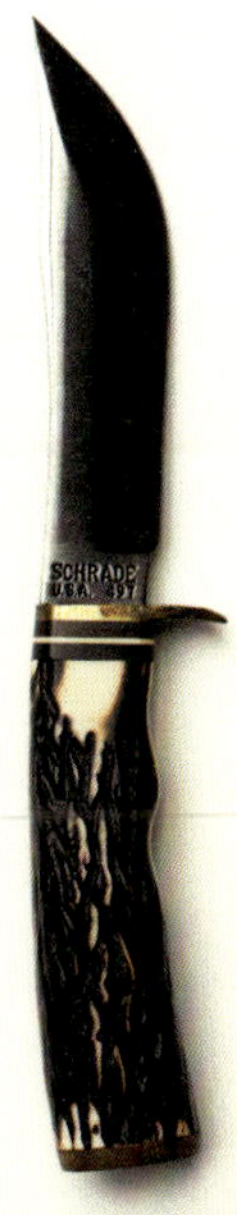

497 Fixed Blade, Schrade-Walden
c. 1976, Wawarsing, NY

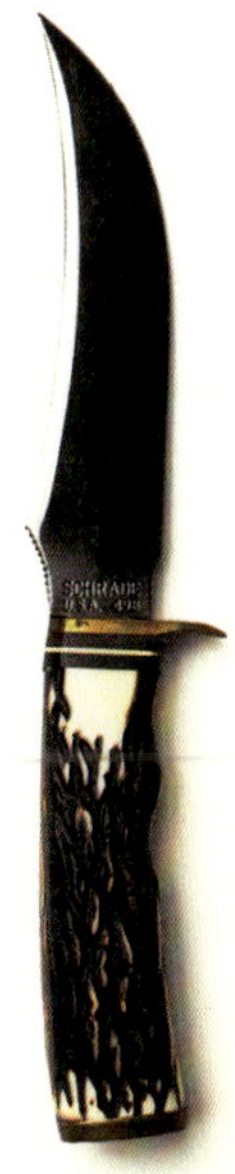

498 Fixed Blade, Schrade-Walden
c. 1977, Wawarsing, NY

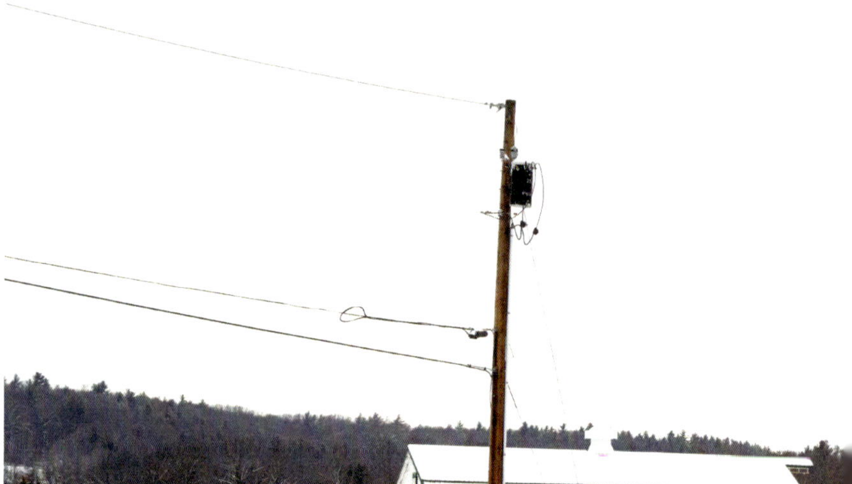

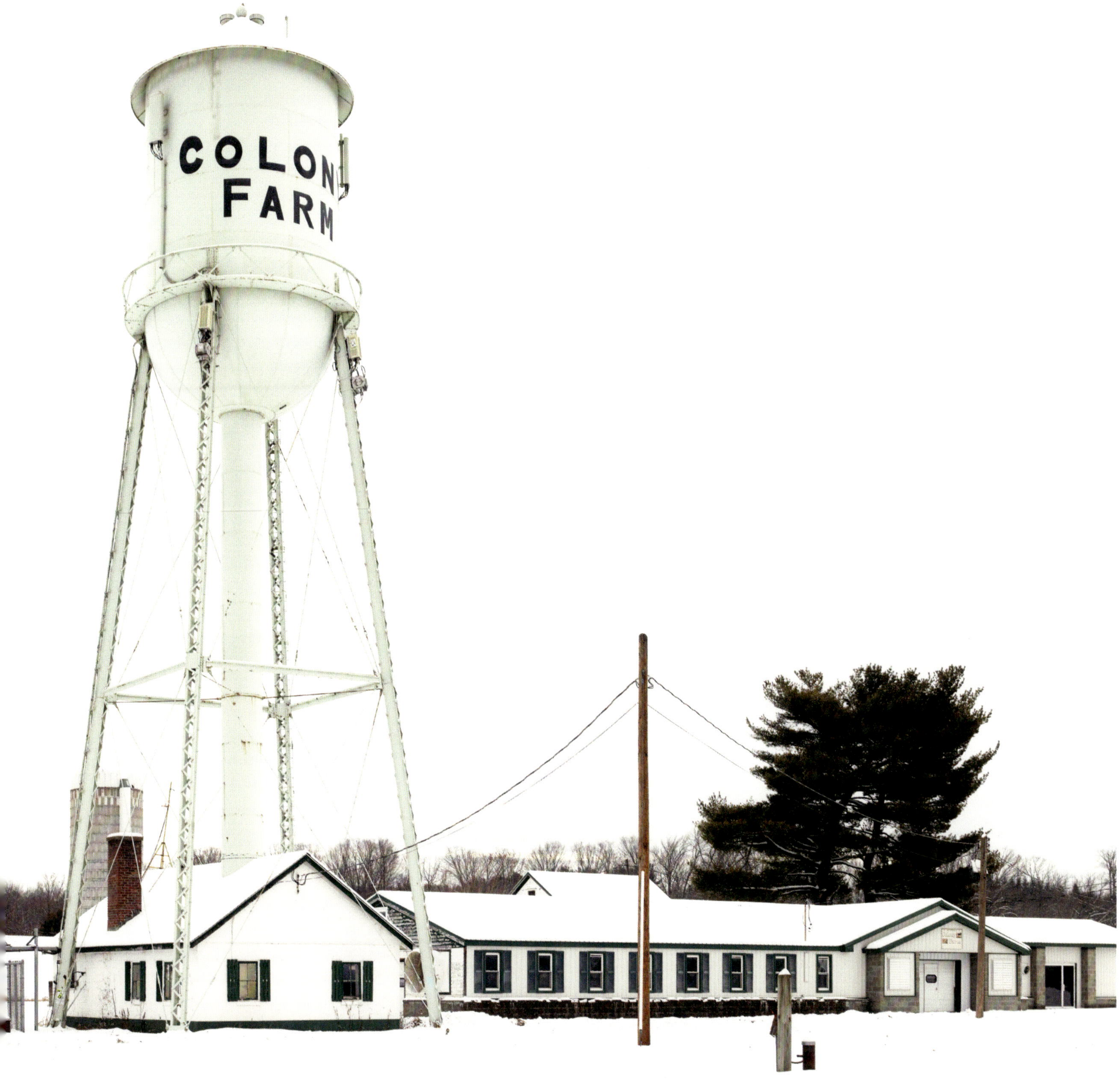
COLON
FARM

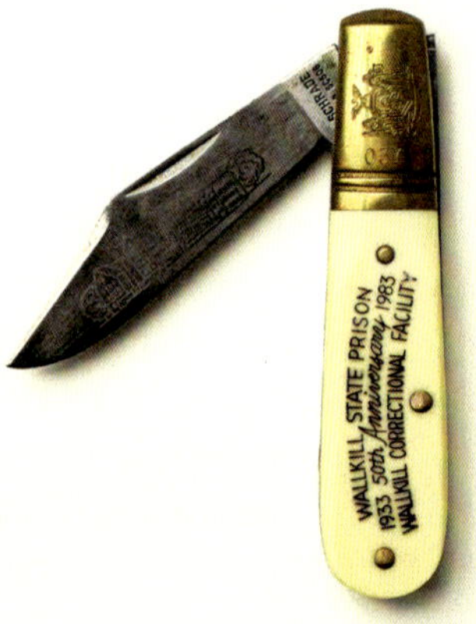

Barlow Scrimshaw, Wallkill 50th Anniversary, Schrade-Walden
1983, Wawarsing, NY

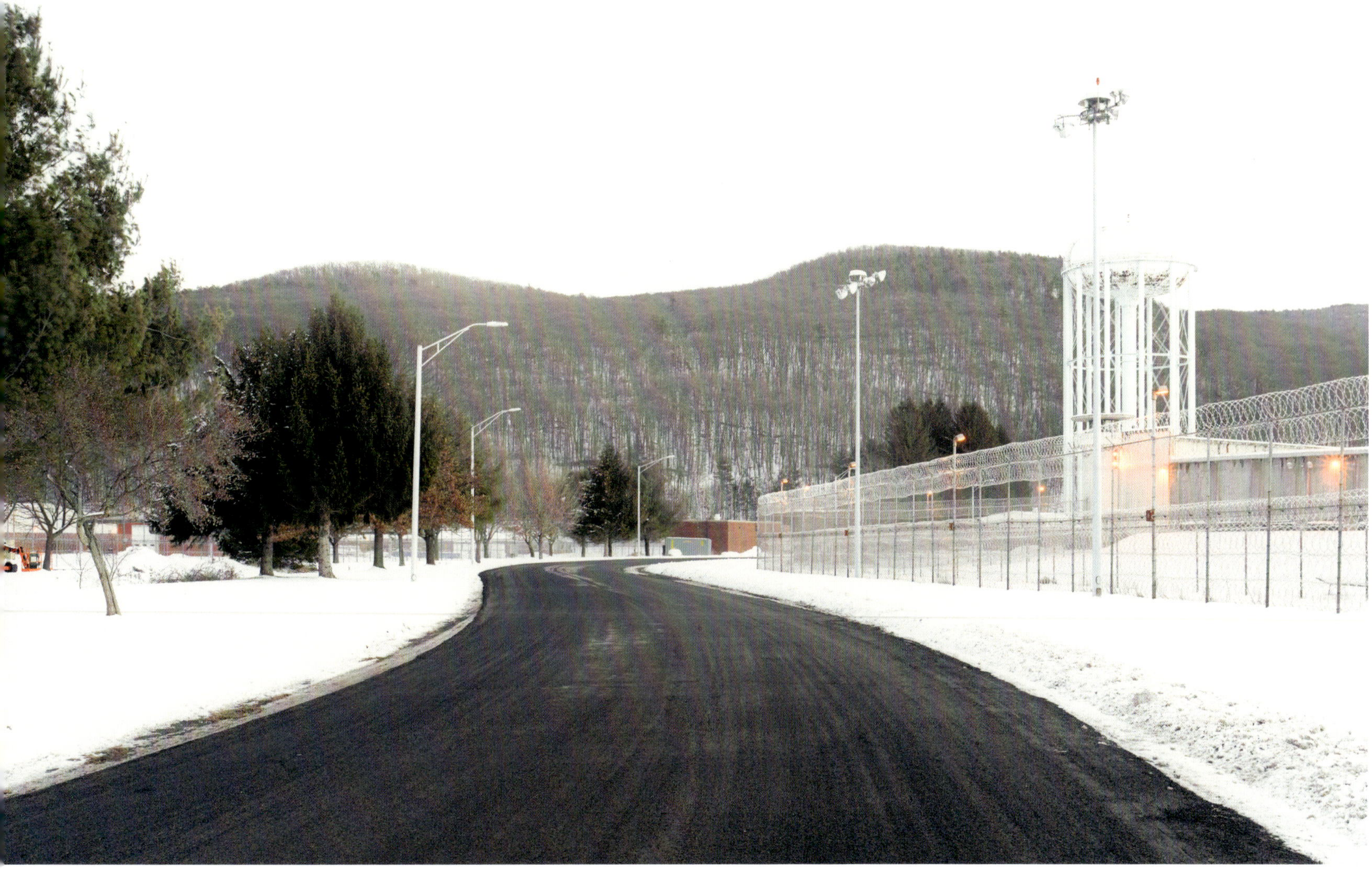

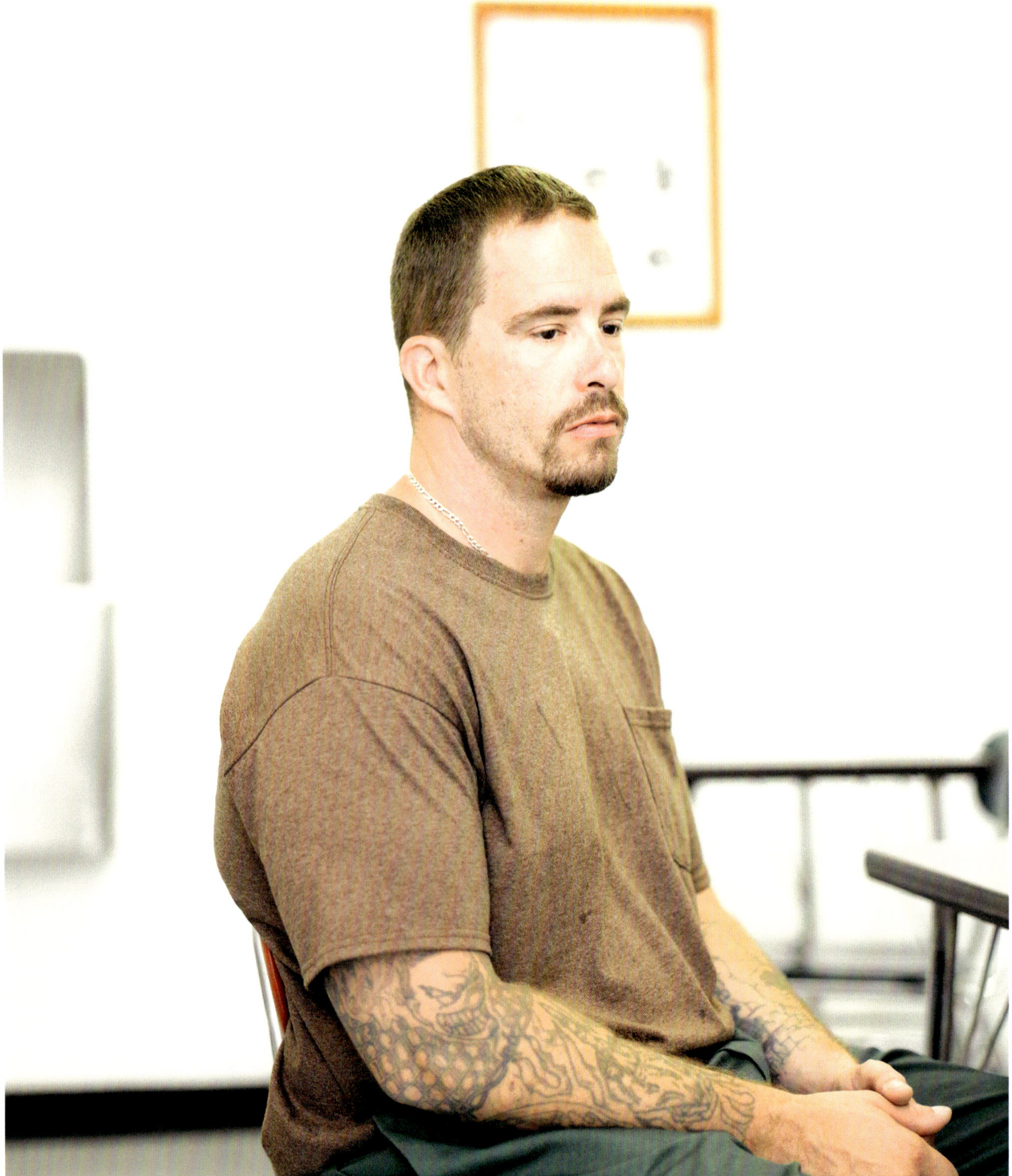

DIN	INMATE NAME	LATEST ADMISSION DATE	ER DATE		CRIME
98A0196	SEWDER, BGARU	1998-01-07	06/19/2024		MURDER/MANSLAUGHTER 1ST
98A0247	ORTIZ, ERLBERT	1998-01-23	09/27/2027		ROBBERY 2ND
98A0982	HARVEY, STGRHGORY	1998-02-03	06/20/2023		MURDER 2ND
98A0985	HADZOCKI, CHARRICE	1998-02-05	06/22/2023		MURDER 2ND
98A1667	PRIMASA, BANDERIN J	1998-02-19	03/20/2024		MURDER 2ND
98A1699	STEELE, WONDEAM R	1998-03-17	03/20/2025		RODMYS 3RD
98A2890	RANSON, RIDNARDLL	1998-04-06	08/08/2029		ROBBERY 1ST
96A0873	MAMERONL, IMERHAEL	1996-04-18	05/20/2029	ATT	MURDER 2ND
96A0874	DANBONY, PARRECK	1996-04-18	09/26/2022		ROBBERY 2ND
96A2180	ERNIS, GANDREW	1996-06-26	09/30/2027		ROBBERY 1ST
96A2369	SUTHERLAND, WARTON	1996-06-08	05/23/2029		ROBBERY 2ND
96A2359	RABERSON, ORCANAEL	1996-06-25	02/18/2020		MURDER 2ND
96A2927	HAVICK, AERANK	1996-06-29	04/26/2028		CRIM POSS CONTR SUBSTANCE 1ST
96A3079	RHODMA, ABUN	1996-06-22	08/17/2019		MANSLAUGHTER 1ST
96A3818	HOZARDANRUANALENTINE	1996-08-02	03/03/2028		ROBBERY 2ND
96A3529	WEARNE, DAMONN	1996-08-18	07/28/2019		ROBBERY 2ND
96A3626	HOBRDEN, VADRDAN	1996-08-27	06/26/2028		MURDER 2ND
96A5442	REEKER, DOMENEY L	1996-08-25	09/30/2021		CRIM POSS STOLEN PROP 3RD
96A4663	WOUNGAMANTROMOTHY	1996-08-28	06/09/2026		MURDER 2ND
96A4685	WENISAMKENNORN	1996-08-30	06/30/2019		BURGLARY 2ND
96A5237	DAREANGIPRANCANTONIO	1996-07-29	11/09/2020		BURGLARY 1ST
96A5922	CAMERSTWEROBNRT	1996-08-24	10/28/2021		ARSON 2ND
96A6131	RAMSBERG, AMATTHEW	1996-09-03	09/26/2029		ROBBERY 2ND
96A6990	GARCIADINIBBAKL	1996-10-26	06/23/2019		RAPE 1ST
96A7289	HUMBERKEDARYHARLES	1996-09-26	09/26/2020	ATT	MURDER 2ND
96A7968	RIVAGN, RODILON	1996-10-08	05/19/2029		CRIM SALE CONTR SUBSTANCE 2ND
96A8277	THOMARD, ADRIAN	1996-10-06	05/20/2018	ATT	MURDER 2ND
96A8748	CORREASTUSHRORINGO	1996-11-17	04/27/2027		MURDER 2ND
96A8458	DRAWNO, MARWINOU	1996-12-20	12/26/2024		ROBBERY 2ND
99A0039	AGUERANS, HEATORN	1999-02-01	07/03/2024		CRIM SALE CONTR SUBSTANCE 3RD
99A0895	ROBINSON, IEVERVIE	1999-02-25	04/23/2027		MURDER 2ND
99A2089	DRAKRODRARIABDULKARIYM M	1999-02-29	04/29/2025		ASSAULT 1ST DEGREE
95A0518	MENDOZA, NDORJOSE	1995-01-30	04/29/2019		MANSLAUGHTER 1ST
95A0836	DAIGREDDY, EDWREAN	1995-03-20	10/16/2021		MURDER 2ND
95A0860	MCARNZIES, ICATIF	1995-06-20	08/20/2020		ROBBERY 2ND
95A0464	CLARKN, MCONABL	1995-08-04	09/16/2028	ATT	MURDER 2ND
95A1208	SANCHEZ, GABANES JR	1995-02-29	05/20/2017		MURDER 2ND
95A1129	BORRES, WHITNEYW	1995-05-06	06/22/2026		MURDER 2ND
95A1222	AHRON, BARRYE	1995-05-22	08/18/2023		MURDER 2ND
95A1969	ROBINA, VONIOR	1995-06-02	09/22/2024		MURDER 2ND
95A2016	RENEZ, JAANFIS	1995-06-06	07/28/2029		MURDER 2ND
95A2043	AHMEDYUNBLEH	1995-04-19	09/30/2029		KIDNAPPING 2ND
95A0159	GANTS, GRONORY	1995-06-19	08/19/2022		MURDER 2ND
95A2406	WRENAAMEDWARDFRERY	1995-06-27	09/26/2029		KIDNAPPING 1ST
95A0896	WALKER, DONNIE	1995-03-21	06/20/2026		BURGLARY 2ND
95A5100	ARAWEIBANEES, JAMES	1995-08-04	07/09/2020		ROBBERY 2ND
95A6164	RATO, VAREON	1995-08-11	07/05/2028		MURDER 2ND
95A6637	DOVEIFRANAAMRE	1995-08-26	04/14/2024	ATT	MURDER 2ND
95A6829	JOHNSON, NTARSEY	1995-08-28	08/02/2025		MURDER 2ND
95A7076	SANDOS, LUTHER	1995-09-09	04/15/2029		MURDER 2ND
95A7870	MORASCASTRVONSANT	1995-09-10	04/20/2016		MANSLAUGHTER 1ST
95A7497	FANCEZ, EVARHAR	1995-10-09	12/23/2027		ROBBERY 1ST
95A7808	MAAZOMEDOMANUEL	1995-10-27	08/04/2029		MURDER 2ND
95A8238	NAUDREN, CHATTHEW	1995-10-25	03/04/2029		MURDER 2ND
95B0655	SANDERS, WALLIAM	1995-10-26	07/25/2029		MURDER 2ND
95B2618	ARNEED, PBAVED	1995-12-20	12/04/2028		MURDER 2ND
96A0537	OCANEN, CHRISTOPHER	1996-01-10	10/16/2027	ATT	MURDER 2ND
96A6058	CHEN, STEVEN	1996-02-14	06/26/2028	ATT	GRAND LARCENY - NOT AUTO 2ND
96A6292	WILLIAMSWIBARAM	1996-02-29	03/31/2020		ROBBERY 1ST
96A6638	GUTIERREZRNOMAR	1996-03-09	06/30/2024		MURDER 2ND
96A6687	GRIFFIN, MICHAEL	1996-03-20	08/20/2024		BURGLARY 2ND
96A0266	MORSLAD, ALBERTO	1996-03-31	10/12/2026		ROBBERY 2ND
96A0889	GARCIA, JESUS C	1996-05-24	04/06/2029		KIDNAPPING 1ST
96A0816	MORELLPS, JOSRUKEJ	1996-04-29	08/07/2020		RAPE 1ST
96A2099	SANCHEZ, DANIELEREYMAN	1996-06-19	08/17/2019		MURDER 2ND
96A3929	MOLINA, ILROBERT	1996-06-27	10/26/2025		MURDER 2ND
98A0156	ARAUJO, CALVIN	1998-06-16	10/08/2020		MURDER 2ND
98A0448	VANDAK, ORLANDON	1998-06-28	01/19/2018		RAPE 1ST
98A0097	MORNORFIJEARRDUR A	1998-02-02	05/06/2023		ASSAULT 1ST DEGREE
98A0596	SIADDROUKEDICHARD	1998-02-07	01/20/2021		ROBBERY 1ST
98A0974	FAULKNER, ARNONALD G	1998-02-28	12/23/2027	ATT	CRIM POSS WEAP 3RD SUB 4-8 VFO
98A1769	NORRIS, NELSON	1998-03-07	03/09/2020	ATT	MURDER 2ND
98A7565	PAGAN, COSMOS, CHRISTIAN	1998-03-06	06/14/2027	ATT	ROBBERY 1ST
98A7021	BARSHTEEN, LMICHAEL	1998-03-23	10/28/2029		MURDER 2ND
98A7882	WILLIAMS, DNGRKESTTON	1998-04-05	10/21/2025		CRIM POSS CONTR SUBSTANCE 3RD
98A7787	ZUNIGA, JUAN	1998-04-08	04/09/2025		KIDNAPPING 1ST
98A8009	GREENLT, RONLEXANDER	1998-04-20	03/07/2018		MANSLAUGHTER 1ST
98A2781	KUMRIELO, JOSEPH	1998-04-23	11/10/2020		ROBBERY 2ND
97A0087	CARIGNAN, CHRISTOPHER	1997-01-26	03/17/2025		MURDER 2ND
97A0447	MALBERY, THOMANCE	1997-01-07	06/14/2025		MURDER 2ND
97A2562	MICHALEK, MICHAEL	1997-01-09	06/14/2027		RAPE 1ST
97A2669	EDWARDS, BRIAN	1997-01-20	07/10/2029		MURDER 2ND
97A2083	CAMARGO, GENEC	1997-02-07	06/29/2026		ROBBERY 2ND
97A2194	MORGAN, ANDREW	1997-02-20	08/20/2022	ATT	BURGLARY 2ND
97A2060	MENCHETTI, FREDERICK	1997-03-16	09/22/2022		CRIM SALE CONTR SUBSTANCE 2ND
97A2881	LEARKAL, TON ON	1997-03-24	06/22/2023		MURDER 2ND
97A3058	ZYMAN, DUANE	1997-06-09	05/09/2027		KIDNAPPING 1ST
97A3149	JENKINS, RUSSELL	1997-06-20	12/26/2019	ATT	MURDER 2ND
97A3691	MCCORL, CARLWAUN	1997-07-23	10/21/2019		MANSLAUGHTER 1ST
97A2780	CASATELLO, CARMINE	1997-07-06	04/11/2020		MURDER 2ND
97A3629	SANDE, SYNELONDRA	1997-07-27	09/23/2029		ROBBERY 2ND
97A4063	DOMINIQUE, RONALD	1997-09-14	05/27/2022	ATT	MURDER 2ND
97A4284	SALINAS, FRANCISCO	1997-09-06	10/31/2023		MURDER 2ND
97A4906	QUINONES, SOSJOSE A	1997-09-30	05/20/2025		MURDER 2ND

DIN	INMATE NAME	LATEST ADMISSION DATE	ER DATE		CRIME
02A5659	RODRIGUEZ, ALMARCOS	2002-04-09	06/22/2028		COURSE SEX CONDUCT-CHILD 1ST
02A6280	GARVER, UDREYT	2002-09-04	06/28/2020		BURGLARY 2ND
02A6795	YOUNG, DEVONN E	2002-08-02	09/26/2028		BURGLARY 1ST
02A6889	ARTIS, ANTWONYA	2002-08-08	08/23/2028		CRIM POSS WEAP 2ND
02A0332	HASMER, DARNEEL LEE	2002-02-06	08/06/2028		MANSLAUGHTER 1ST
02A0974	VANBECK, MARICHARD T	2002-10-09	05/29/2028		MANSLAUGHTER 1ST
02A0639	HRENADEZ, SCARIS M	2002-09-15	06/05/2025		ROBBERY 2ND
02A0799	RODRIGUEZ, XUAVIER	2002-02-18	04/15/2028		MANSLAUGHTER 1ST
02A0268	RACHLEDORANLOUIS	2002-02-14	08/05/2022	ATT	ROBBERY 2ND
02A8329	HEVENDEZARANMONIO	2002-06-24	11/29/2026		MURDER 2ND
02A8649	SRAWSEW, RORMEN	2002-07-29	02/06/2028	ATT	ROBBERY 2ND
02A8638	DOGNL, GREGHARD M	2002-08-35	08/28/2028		MANSLAUGHTER 1ST
03A0028	COVAR, MACHAEL	2003-02-07	08/18/2024		ROBBERY 2ND
03A0779	HOATARDDONRAD A	2003-02-13	03/28/2030		CRIM SALE FIREARM 1ST-DEG
03A0270	EDREN, LDAVERY	2003-02-22	08/18/2026		GRAND LARCENY - AUTO 4TH
03A0987	MURRAY, AARON	2003-03-04	04/25/2028		MANSLAUGHTER 1ST
03A0987	BENAW, FRANKER	2003-03-01	09/08/2019		MANSLAUGHTER 1ST
03A1727	LAREZOMENDEZAOLMAAME	2003-04-07	10/06/2022		MURDER 2ND
03A1082	PLEVGER, TMICHAEL S	2003-04-24	07/28/2029		MANSLAUGHTER 1ST
03A2276	EMANUEL, CHRDARREN	2003-05-02	10/23/2028		MANSLAUGHTER 1ST
03A2992	GOMESTRUZ, AWYBRIAN	2003-05-25	08/03/2023		MANSLAUGHTER 1ST
03A2698	MAMIAR, NEBSON	2003-05-20	09/06/2029		ROBBERY 1ST
03A2466	CARTER, DNAARONEAL	2003-05-29	08/28/2019		MANSLAUGHTER 1ST
03A2869	BERGSS, MARBORTA	2003-06-10	05/10/2030		CRIM SEXUAL ACT 1ST
03A2838	NARESHEWANEJOSEPH	2003-06-15	06/08/2025		ROBBERY 2ND
03A3702	TVSRKJ, SMARNANL	2003-06-28	08/09/2030		CRIM SALE CONTR SUBSTANCE 3RD
03A3867	GARSND, HAOHN	2003-06-25	10/02/2026		ASSAULT 2ND
03A3959	WOODINGTON, KIEMAEL	2003-06-26	09/14/2027		RAPE 1ST
03A3961	AEDAN, MADALINE	2003-06-26	07/27/2025		MURDER 2ND
03A2428	COLIBU, VONCENT	2003-07-05	10/26/2025		BURGLARY 1ST
03A3086	HANSACHJOHNRANCE	2003-07-06	08/30/2025	ATT	ROBBERY 2ND
03A3939	DAVIS, DHAWNTE L	2003-07-29	05/28/2020		ROBBERY 1ST
03A3868	GANADAMARWINSTON	2003-08-10	12/16/2029		MURDER 2ND
03A2988	AYALA, ANTHONY	2003-08-10	10/25/2022	ATT	BURGLARY 2ND
03A0695	ADMOMANLIWALTER	2003-08-18	11/28/2027	ATT	MURDER 2ND
03A0786	GOMEZ, GUEZAEANTONIO D	2003-08-20	12/05/2029		COURSE SEX CONDUCT-CHILD 1ST
03A5580	SAVANANGHMARQUISE	2003-07-15	07/27/2024	ATT	BURGLARY 2ND
03A6079	WILLIAMS, LOVELAND	2003-07-26	10/04/2027		CRIM POSS CONTR SUBSTANCE 1ST
03A6475	MARTINEZ, RRICETOR	2003-08-08	12/06/2027		MANSLAUGHTER 1ST
03A6707	DCASLO, MIRUMENL	2003-08-02	06/26/2020	ATT	ROBBERY 1ST
03A6718	GAVASRA, JUANVALDO	2003-08-25	02/04/2028		CRIM SALE FIREARM 1ST-DEG
03A6867	YANNGZ, SHANMIAEL	2003-08-16	11/25/2029		ROBBERY 2ND
03A6975	MURLLIVANJANAAN	2003-09-29	06/19/2021	ATT	CRIM SEXUAL ACT 1ST
03A4926	QUINONES, GOCHRISTIAN	2003-09-28	08/06/2028	ATT	ASSAULT 1ST DEGREE
03A6022	LOPEZ-ROMERO, GABRIEL A	2003-09-26	03/07/2028		KIDNAPPING 1ST
03A6606	AHMEDSONAMAASNEEM	2003-09-26	04/28/2027		MANSLAUGHTER 1ST
03A6576	PEREIRA, ALFREDO	2003-09-30	02/20/2023	ATT	MANSLAUGHTER 1ST
03A5565	HERNANDEZ, JEFFERSON	2003-10-02	09/05/2029		ASSAULT 1ST DEGREE
03A5858	MERCADO, JOHNSON	2003-10-07	08/06/2023		MANSLAUGHTER 1ST
03A5160	MARANONZ, MIGDONY	2003-10-08	09/22/2029		MANSLAUGHTER 1ST
03A5198	RANDCEANTIPETER	2003-10-02	03/26/2029		MURDER 2ND
03A5404	RODRIGUEZ, RODRIGUEZ, RAFAEL	2003-12-05	12/07/2023		KIDNAPPING 2ND
03A5495	GODEEY, MASON D	2003-12-08	02/09/2027		CRIM POSS CONTR SUBSTANCE 3RD
03A5668	FREEMAN, CDARREN R	2003-12-06	06/28/2022	ATT	BURGLARY 2ND
03A6580	WATSON, HOWARD	2003-12-13	06/08/2020	ATT	BURGLARY 2ND
03A6661	SMAREST, HILARY	2003-12-20	10/27/2029		MANSLAUGHTER 1ST
03A6792	OORERO, DREAMPE	2003-12-29	09/15/2024		ROBBERY 1ST
03A6939	TRUMKRTROMANIE	2003-12-30	04/08/2020		MURDER 2ND
03B0186	SUNDBERGENORRIJOSEPH M	2003-01-20	10/28/2026		COURSE SEX CONDUCT-CHILD 1ST
03B0899	TORRENTINOFFRENARD J	2003-02-19	08/14/2027		CRIM POSS CONTR SUBSTANCE 3RD
03B1420	BONERN, MICHAEL	2003-05-09	06/02/2019		ASSAULT 1ST DEGREE
03B2280	VASQUEZ, ANGEL A	2003-07-17	10/12/2027		BURGLARY 2ND
04A0274	SPOTARDS, SHEDWARD	2004-02-22	05/29/2029		CRIM SEXUAL ACT 1ST
04A0467	THOMAS, KAQUON	2004-02-04	08/11/2020	ATT	ASSAULT 1ST DEGREE
04A0175	BRADFORD, TRAVOR	2004-02-13	09/09/2029	ATT	MURDER 2ND
04A0935	HARVEY, MICHAEL E	2004-02-19	04/16/2026		KIDNAPPING 2ND
04A1289	ALEXANDER, WILLIAMPAEL	2004-03-28	11/12/2029	ATT	MURDER 2ND
04A1261	HAWKINS, JAMALIK	2004-03-26	03/24/2021		BURGLARY 2ND
04A1495	HEATON, CARLOS, ELOR	2004-03-27	07/28/2019		ROBBERY 1ST
04A1498	WHITEHEAD, SHEDRET	2004-03-26	10/09/2023		CRIM POSS CONTR SUBSTANCE 3RD
04A1567	HOWARD, EMICHAEL J	2004-03-31	08/31/2028	ATT	ARSON 2ND
04A1797	MANNISH, CLINTON D	2004-03-22	09/11/2026		CRIM POSS WEAP 2ND
04A1908	DIXON, AUDHN	2004-02-09	06/22/2027		MANSLAUGHTER 1ST
04A2025	FRANCIS, KHALIEF	2004-02-12	04/14/2025		BURGLARY 2ND
04A2584	DEAORSE, CHARLES	2004-04-15	03/15/2026		CONSPIRACY 2ND
04A2779	STOUNDRIGNACASTILLO, RAMON	2004-04-15	10/16/2022	ATT	MURDER 2ND
04A2869	HUNCARD, ABERNARDO	2004-04-27	04/25/2028		CRIM POSS CONTR SUBSTANCE 1ST
04A2896	GUARASVESSORASON	2004-05-01	10/28/2026		BURGLARY 2ND
04A2918	HINTON, ANDINGEDJUAN	2004-04-02	12/28/2025		ROBBERY 2ND
04A5054	CONSTANTINE, CHRISTOPHER C	2004-06-05	10/27/2026	ATT	BURGLARY 2ND
04A3276	CAMPOS, SLANDLYCOLM	2004-06-26	09/18/2028		CRIM POSS WEAP 2ND
04A3249	OCTAVARES, NTDANIEL	2004-06-13	08/09/2029		BURGLARY 1ST
04A3562	HERNANDEZ, KENNETH	2004-06-29	12/16/2029		CONSPIRACY 2ND
04A3517	WASHINGTON, LTJAMES	2004-07-13	11/25/2020		MANSLAUGHTER 1ST
04A3126	PARKER, KEVIN	2004-07-13	10/17/2019	ATT	BURGLARY 1ST
04A3429	THOMPSON, CALBERT	2004-07-14	09/29/2026		MANSLAUGHTER 1ST
04A3156	MALDONADO, NHAALIX	2004-07-25	08/05/2022	ATT	ASSAULT 1ST DEGREE
04A4248	THOMAS, ANTHONY	2004-07-20	07/18/2025	ATT	CONSPIRACY 2ND
04A4423	MARCORD, WALCTRAVIS	2004-08-29	07/26/2028	ATT	COURSE SEX CONDUCT-CHILD 1ST
04A4298	BARNES, AISLAY	2004-09-24	12/29/2019		BURGLARY 2ND
04A4285	RAYMOND, URBRIAN	2004-09-24	10/25/2027		BURGLARY 2ND
04A5347	RAYMOND, TSHADDMAEL	2004-09-27	01/10/2019		MANSLAUGHTER 1ST
04A5595	HERNANDEZ, FERNANDO	2004-09-02	07/25/2027		ROBBERY 1ST
04A5565	SANCHEZ, JORGE	2004-06-25	05/05/2024		MANSLAUGHTER 1ST

DIN	INMATE NAME	LATEST ADMISSION DATE
02A5648	RODRIGUEZ, ROBERT JR	2002-10-29
02A6204	GARCIA, VEJOSMARCELINO	2002-12-09
02A6211	CEARR, BRYAN	2002-12-04
02A6207	GRAHAM, DANTHONY	2002-12-14
02A6722	MARTINEZ, YRAMIREL	2002-12-06
02A4914	AMERY, MARKOLPH	2002-10-08
02A4670	HERNANDEZ, CARTER D	2003-01-15
02A4774	RODRIGUEZ, RODRAVIER	2002-12-30
02A8709	BRAUGRADDOMNLOUIS	2002-12-16
02A8126	HERNANDEZ, ALANTONIO	2002-11-20
02A1439	BROWN, JEROMEY	2002-07-16
02A1086	HERNANDEZ, RICHARD M	2002-08-18
03A0038	ROYAER, JACKSHON	2003-03-08
03A0329	DORAN, CHRISTOPHER	2003-03-31
03A1270	MATELLES, ROBERT	2003-04-06
03A1287	WARFIELD, LARONALD JR	2003-04-07
03A1982	DANAS, FERMINRIUS	2003-04-16
03A0002	HERNANDEZ, MALCOLM	2003-04-07
03A0077	RIVERA, TYRELL	2003-04-24
03A2226	EMANUEL, EDDARREN	2003-05-06
03A2926	MENDEZ, JERMAIN	2003-05-13
03A2942	MONTERO, KELVIN	2003-05-26
03A2606	CARIOPE, AARONE	2003-05-28
03A2944	BRIDGE, ROBERT	2003-06-14
03A2939	RYAN, THOMANNJOSEPH	2003-06-10
03A3368	IVERY, TINJAKOBIN	2003-06-26
03A3443	MARKLIN, ADENNIS D	2003-06-19
03A3246	WOLDINGTON, PENELOPE	2003-06-27
03A3261	AUCOBA, SHARAMTIAN	2003-06-24
03A3429	ORDONEZ, KENEIL	2003-07-03
03A3496	CANITERVERN ERICK	2003-07-08
03A3566	DAVISON, SHAWNE	2003-07-08
03A3580	SAIADANAR, JONATHAN	2003-07-18
03A3980	AYAKO, TANSON	2003-07-28
03A4015	MACWAN, KENNAALTONN	2003-08-02
03A4370	RODRIGUEZ, ANTONIO D	2003-08-26
03A4398	EDISON, MOMARQUISE	2003-09-27
03A4407	UZARDEREL, EYROLAND	2003-10-04
03A4604	MARTINEZ, GOINESTOR	2003-10-06
03A4694	GOADREY, RUBMOND	2003-11-04
03A4815	MALDONA, DAVID DO	2003-11-02
03A4939	SANCHEZ, JUMICHAEL	2003-11-10
03A4819	GOMEZ, MARMANRITO	2003-12-22
03A4910	QUINONES, EDCHRISTIAN	2003-12-21
03A4822	KALZ, EYEDWARD	2003-12-27
03A1046	ANDERSON, RASHREEK	2003-05-29
03B1060	WALEFIANTHONY W	2003-07-30
05A0351	HERNANDEZ, VISEG	2005-09-29
05A0154	ROUSMAN, JOBERT	2005-10-07
05A5278	MARTINEZ, CRMIGUEL	2005-10-03
05A5992	MAQUILAHESTEBAN	2005-10-02
05A5442	HERNANDEZ, GONZALEZ, RAFAEL	2005-10-13
05A1098	DUDNEY, ROBERT	2005-10-17
05A4261	PEREZ, LAANTHONY	2005-12-08
05A4623	MURPHY, NICHOLAS	2005-12-20
05A4688	HOLGUIN, GUSTAVO	2005-12-28
05A4752	OLIVARO, JERRYPE	2005-12-23
05A4019	ARCANGEL, UNOMANESAR	2005-03-27
05A1800	PONTO, EDUARDS	2005-06-18
05A1297	SORRENTINO, BERNARD J	2005-08-08
05A2608	MORUEG, JASON	2005-09-09
05A2367	REDDICK, SGABRIEL A	2005-09-27
06A0290	EDWARDS, BRANDWARD	2006-05-20
06A0267	BARONE, MAGDON	2006-02-20
06A0927	ARKURRAD, BRYAN	2006-02-31
06A0932	MIRANDA, MEDUARDO	2006-02-09
06A1289	ANDRADE, TOALLANFAEL	2006-03-08
06A3997	GAFFEY, JARURV	2006-03-28
06A1483	BRATHOWN, CHANCELLOR	2006-03-28
06A3099	MEDINA, LUCHNNY	2006-03-16
06A5582	MONEAU, BRUCE	2006-03-29
06A5725	HARPER, MOHAMMED	2006-03-29
06A5973	NOVEL, ANTOFI	2006-04-05
06A9069	WATKINS, DAVID	2006-04-18
06A9476	SANLEY, CHARLES	2006-04-16
06A9476	STROM, GORAND	2006-04-16
06A9900	GRANOR, AABDUL K	2006-04-27
06A2884	DUBNAR, UICFREDERICK	2006-05-07
06A2998	ALEVESTAND, INANGUAN	2006-06-09
06A5076	BOWMAN, EIVYRONNARD	2006-06-05
06A5089	BRAND, STANLEY	2006-06-18
06A5745	RODRIGUES, GABRIEL	2006-06-24
06A5874	ADSERU, PEDMOND	2006-06-25
06A5584	WASHINGTON, JAMES	2006-07-07
06A5966	MARLENDONOMKAMAR	2006-07-08
06A5888	ENCARNACION, GABRIEL	2006-07-09
06A5020	MALDONADO, NOELIX	2006-07-08
06A6042	MOORE, ANTHONY	2006-07-20
06A6089	BAIRD, STOKANT	2006-08-20
06A8888	BARNES, JDONALD	2006-08-14
06A8883	HARRISON, BURTON W JR	2006-08-14
06A8949	MAHONEY, IAMICHAEL	2006-09-07
06A8596	HERNANDEZ, EDUARDO	2006-09-30
06A5580	SANCHEZ, DAGOBANE JOSE	2006-10-05

ER DATE		CRIME

DIN	INMATE NAME	LATEST ADMISSION DATE	ER DATE		CRIME

DIN	INMATE NAME	LATEST ADMISSION DATE	ER DATE		CRIME

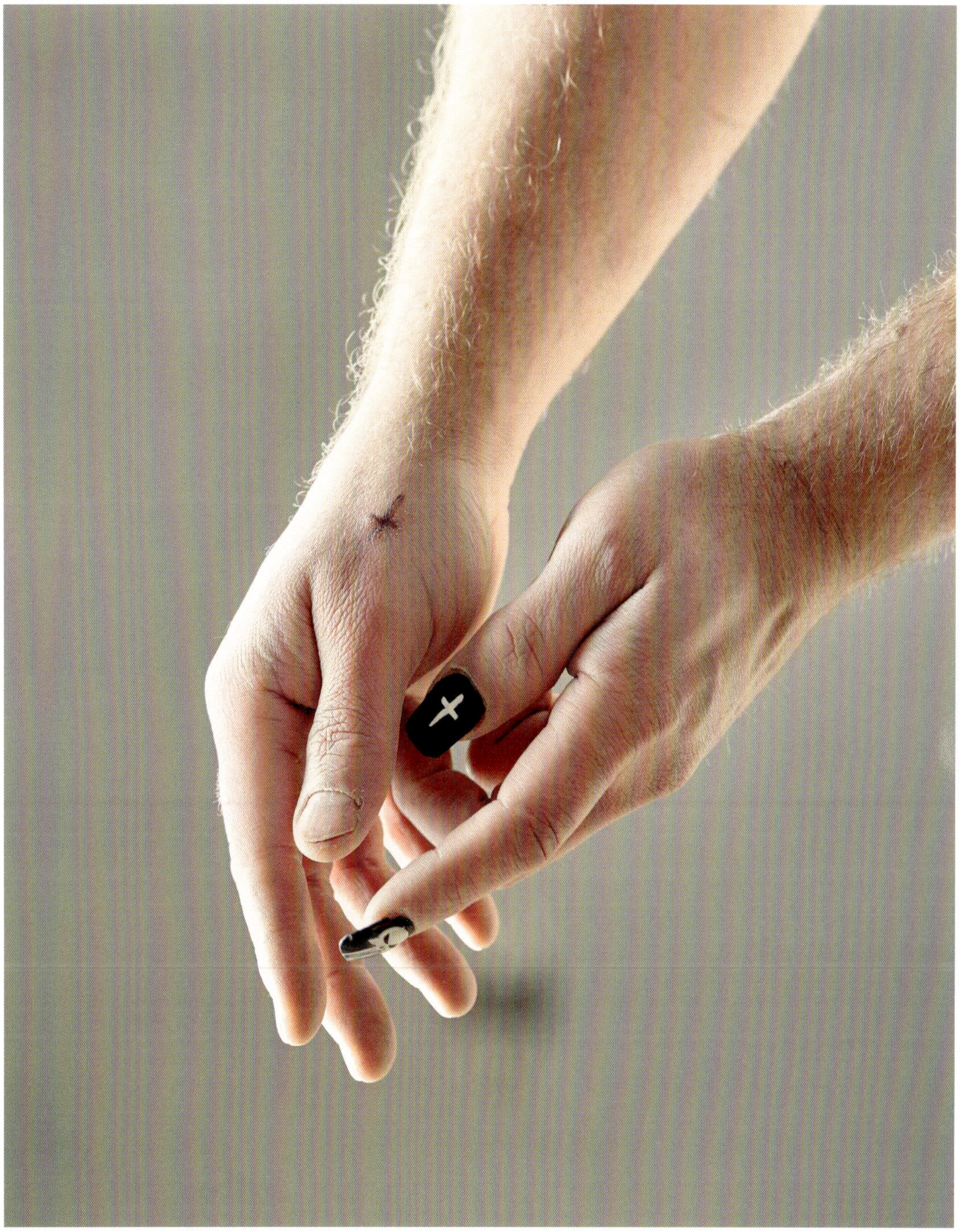

DIN	INMATE NAME	LATEST ADMISSION DATE	ER DATE	CRIME
02A0165	[illegible]CARLAS, JOSE	2002-04-07	06/10/2026	[illegible] CONDUCT-CHILD 1ST
02A0947	[illegible]	2002-04-11	10/21/2028	[illegible] 2ND
02A0642	[illegible]	[illegible]	06/20/2026	MURDER 2ND
02A0546	[illegible]	[illegible]	04/20/2028	[illegible]ER 1ST
02A1987	[illegible]	2002-05-15	[illegible]	[illegible] 1ST
02A1989	[illegible]	2002-05-17	[illegible]	[illegible]REPORTING INCIDENT-2ND
02A2099	[illegible]	2002-06-06	07/08/2028	[illegible] 1ST
02A2129	CAMERON, [illegible]	2002-06-10	05/29/2028	MURDER 2ND
02A2174	[illegible]AME N	2002-06-18	10/12/2021	ASSAULT 1ST DEGREE
02A2182	[illegible]LIO A	2002-06-26	04/18/2020	[illegible] 1ST
02A2285	[illegible]	2002-05-29	[illegible]	ROBBERY 1ST
02A2759	[illegible]	2002-05-25	02/03/2020	ATT [illegible] 2ND
02A2963	[illegible]	2002-06-04	09/24/2028	[illegible] SUBSTANCE 1ST
02A3624	[illegible]	2002-06-12	09/17/2026	[illegible] 1ST
02A3618	[illegible]	2002-07-07	10/21/2020	ASSAULT 1ST DEGREE
02A3701	[illegible]	2002-07-21	[illegible]	[illegible]EAP 2ND
02A3820	[illegible]TAN	2002-07-22	[illegible]	[illegible]
02A4464	[illegible]	[illegible]	05/25/2021	[illegible] STOLEN PROP 3RD
02A4461	[illegible], ANTHONY	2002-09-08	06/07/2026	[illegible] ACT 1ST
02A4623	LEWIS, [illegible]	[illegible]	[illegible]	ATT [illegible]
02A5054	[illegible]ISCO	[illegible]	10/31/2028	[illegible]
02A5122	[illegible]	[illegible]	[illegible]	[illegible] 2ND
02A5633	[illegible]	2002-12-19	09/26/2023	[illegible] 1ST DEGREE
02A5698	[illegible], MARCOS A	2002-12-29	06/21/2029	RAPE 1ST
02A5705	[illegible]	[illegible]	09/28/2020	ATT [illegible] 2ND
02A5767	[illegible] T	[illegible]	[illegible]	[illegible] ACT 1ST
02A6097	[illegible]	[illegible]	[illegible]	ATT [illegible] 2ND
02A6152	[illegible]DOMINGO	[illegible]	[illegible]	[illegible] 1ST
02A6666	[illegible]	2002-11-20	08/28/2024	[illegible]
02A6822	[illegible]	[illegible]	[illegible]	[illegible]
02A6840	[illegible]	[illegible]	04/25/2026	[illegible]DEFRAUD 1ST
02A7226	[illegible]	[illegible]	[illegible]	ATT [illegible] DEGREE
02A0525	[illegible]	[illegible]	06/29/2029	[illegible] 1ST
02A0636	[illegible]	[illegible]	[illegible]	[illegible] ACT 2ND
02A0864	[illegible]	[illegible]	06/08/2029	[illegible] 1ST
02A0886	[illegible]	[illegible]	[illegible]	[illegible] 1ST
02A4236	[illegible]	[illegible]	[illegible]023	[illegible] 1ST
[illegible]	[illegible]CO	[illegible]	[illegible]	[illegible]EAP 2ND
02A6732	[illegible]	[illegible]	10/16/2025	[illegible] 1ST
02A5997	[illegible]TH	[illegible]	08/12/2026	[illegible]
[illegible]	[illegible]	[illegible]	12/12/2024	ATT [illegible] DEGREE
[illegible]	[illegible]YMOND	[illegible]	[illegible]	[illegible]
[illegible]	[illegible]	[illegible]	02/12/2029	ATT MURDER 2ND
[illegible]	[illegible]	[illegible]	[illegible]	ATT [illegible]EAP 2ND
[illegible]	[illegible]	[illegible]	11/22/2028	BURGLARY 2ND
[illegible]	[illegible] JAMES	[illegible]	[illegible]	[illegible] SUBSTANCE 1ST
[illegible]	[illegible]PH M	[illegible]	07/26/2026	[illegible]SAULT AGAINST CHILD
[illegible]	[illegible]	[illegible]	06/14/2029	ATT [illegible] ACT 1ST
[illegible]	JOHNSON, [illegible]	[illegible]	[illegible]	[illegible]
[illegible]	[illegible] A	[illegible]	[illegible]	[illegible]
[illegible]	[illegible]	[illegible]	[illegible]018	MANSLAUGHTER 1ST
01A6627	[illegible]	[illegible]	05/22/2021	[illegible] 1ST
[illegible]	[illegible] RUBIN	[illegible]	08/04/2029	[illegible]
[illegible]	[illegible]	[illegible]	[illegible]	ATT [illegible] DEGREE
[illegible]	[illegible]	[illegible]	12/18/2028	[illegible] ACT 1ST
[illegible]	[illegible]	[illegible]	[illegible]	[illegible]
[illegible]	[illegible]OPHER	[illegible]	12/18/2022	ATT [illegible]EAP 2ND
[illegible]	[illegible]	[illegible]	[illegible]	ATT [illegible]
[illegible]	[illegible]	[illegible]	07/31/2020	[illegible]
[illegible]	[illegible]	[illegible]	[illegible]	[illegible] DEGREE
[illegible]	[illegible]	[illegible]	[illegible]	ATT [illegible] ACT 1ST
[illegible]	[illegible]	[illegible]	[illegible]	ASSAULT 1ST DEGREE
[illegible]	[illegible]	[illegible]	[illegible]	[illegible] 1ST
[illegible]	[illegible]	[illegible]	[illegible]	[illegible]
[illegible]	[illegible] T	[illegible]	10/17/2027	MURDER 2ND
[illegible]	[illegible]	[illegible]	[illegible]	MURDER 2ND
[illegible]	[illegible]	[illegible]	[illegible]	ATT [illegible]
[illegible]	[illegible] N	[illegible]	[illegible]	[illegible] 1ST DEGREE
[illegible]	[illegible]	[illegible]	[illegible]	ATT [illegible] DEGREE
[illegible]	[illegible]	[illegible]	[illegible]023	[illegible] 2ND DEGREE
[illegible]	[illegible]	[illegible]	[illegible]	ATT [illegible] SUB 4-8 VFO
[illegible]	[illegible]HEW	[illegible]	[illegible]	ATT [illegible]
[illegible]	[illegible], THOMAS	[illegible]	[illegible]	ATT [illegible] DEGREE
[illegible]	[illegible]	[illegible]	[illegible]	ATT [illegible]
[illegible]	[illegible]	[illegible]	[illegible]	[illegible] CONDUCT-CHILD 1ST
[illegible]	[illegible]	[illegible]	[illegible]	[illegible]
[illegible]	[illegible]ANDER	[illegible]	[illegible]	MANSLAUGHTER 1ST
[illegible]	[illegible]	[illegible]	[illegible]	[illegible] DEGREE
[illegible]	[illegible]VIN	[illegible]	[illegible]	[illegible]
[illegible]	[illegible]	[illegible]	[illegible]	[illegible]ER 1ST
[illegible]	[illegible]OPHER	[illegible]	[illegible]	[illegible] DEGREE
[illegible]	[illegible]	[illegible]	[illegible]	[illegible]
[illegible]	[illegible] S	[illegible]	[illegible]	[illegible]
[illegible]	[illegible]	[illegible]	[illegible]	ATT [illegible]
[illegible]	[illegible] V	[illegible]	[illegible]	[illegible]
[illegible]	[illegible]	[illegible]	[illegible]	[illegible]EAP 2ND
[illegible]	[illegible]	[illegible]	[illegible]	[illegible] DEGREE
[illegible]	[illegible]	[illegible]	[illegible]	[illegible]
[illegible]	[illegible] D	[illegible]	[illegible]	ATT [illegible] 1ST
[illegible]	[illegible]MINE	[illegible]	[illegible]	[illegible]
[illegible]	[illegible] JR	[illegible]	[illegible]	[illegible] DEGREE
[illegible]	[illegible]	[illegible]	[illegible]	ATT [illegible]
[illegible]	[illegible]CISCO	[illegible]	[illegible]	ATT [illegible] CONTR SUBSTANCE 3RD
[illegible]	[illegible]	[illegible]	[illegible]	[illegible] CONTR SUBSTANCE 3RD

DIN	INMATE NAME	LATEST ADMISSION DATE	ER DATE	CRIME
[illegible]	[illegible]	[illegible]	05/04/2021	[illegible] 2ND DEGREE
[illegible]	[illegible]CARDO S	[illegible]	09/29/2028	[illegible] SUBSTANCE 1ST
[illegible]	[illegible]	[illegible]	[illegible]	ATT [illegible]
[illegible]	[illegible]	[illegible]	08/26/2024	MANSLAUGHTER 1ST
[illegible]	[illegible]	[illegible]	[illegible]	ATT [illegible]
[illegible]	[illegible]DIS	[illegible]	[illegible]	[illegible]CT-CHILD 1ST
[illegible]	[illegible] JOSE	[illegible]	[illegible]	ATT [illegible] 1ST
[illegible]	[illegible]	[illegible]	[illegible]	[illegible] 1ST DEGREE
[illegible]	[illegible]	[illegible]	10/10/2022	ATT CRIM [illegible] 1ST
[illegible]	[illegible]	[illegible]	[illegible]	[illegible] 1ST
[illegible]	[illegible] T	[illegible]	[illegible]	[illegible] 1ST
[illegible]	[illegible] C	[illegible]	05/23/2029	[illegible] SUBSTANCE 4TH
[illegible]	[illegible]	[illegible]	09/17/2027	[illegible] CONDUCT-CHILD 1ST
[illegible]	[illegible] R	[illegible]	[illegible]	[illegible]
[illegible]	[illegible]	[illegible]	[illegible]	RAPE 1ST
[illegible]	[illegible] N	[illegible]	[illegible]	[illegible]EAP 2ND
[illegible]	[illegible]OPHER L	[illegible]	[illegible]	[illegible]
[illegible]	[illegible]	[illegible]	[illegible]	[illegible]TER 1ST
[illegible]	[illegible] K	[illegible]	[illegible]	[illegible]STANCE 3RD
[illegible]	[illegible] J	[illegible]	[illegible]	ATT [illegible]
[illegible]	[illegible]	[illegible]	[illegible]	CRIM POSS WEAP 2ND
[illegible]	[illegible] HARRY JR	[illegible]	11/25/2028	ATT [illegible]
[illegible]	[illegible]	[illegible]	[illegible]	ATT ROBBERY 2ND
[illegible]	[illegible] LLOYD	[illegible]	[illegible]	[illegible]EAP 2ND
[illegible]	[illegible]	[illegible]	[illegible]	[illegible]
[illegible]	[illegible]TIAN	[illegible]	[illegible]	[illegible]
[illegible]	[illegible]	[illegible]	[illegible]	[illegible]MARIHUANA 1ST
[illegible]	[illegible] A	[illegible]	[illegible]	[illegible] CONTR SUBSTANCE 3RD
[illegible]	[illegible]RICHARD	[illegible]	[illegible]	ATT [illegible]TUTION 3RD
[illegible]	[illegible]	[illegible]	[illegible]	[illegible]FIREARM 1ST-DEG
[illegible]	[illegible]	[illegible]	[illegible]	RAPE 1ST
[illegible]	[illegible]	[illegible]	11/14/2016	[illegible] 1ST
[illegible]	[illegible] M	[illegible]	[illegible]	ATT [illegible] DEGREE
[illegible]	[illegible] L	[illegible]	[illegible]	[illegible]
[illegible]	[illegible]	[illegible]	[illegible]	[illegible]SEXUAL ASSAULT
[illegible]	[illegible]WILLIAM	[illegible]	[illegible]	[illegible]AP 2ND
[illegible]	[illegible]	[illegible]	[illegible]	ATT [illegible] 1ST DEGREE
[illegible]	[illegible]	[illegible]	12/25/2020	[illegible] 1ST
[illegible]	[illegible] H	[illegible]	[illegible]	[illegible]CT-CHILD 1ST
[illegible]	[illegible] J	[illegible]	[illegible]	[illegible] ACT 1ST
[illegible]	[illegible] SR	[illegible]	01/14/2024	[illegible]AULT AGAINST CHILD
[illegible]	[illegible]NTONIO	[illegible]	[illegible]	CONSPIRACY 2ND
[illegible]	[illegible]	[illegible]	[illegible]	[illegible] PROP 4TH
[illegible]	[illegible] JR	[illegible]	02/08/2021	[illegible] SUBSTANCE 2ND
[illegible]	[illegible]WILLIE	[illegible]	[illegible]	ATT [illegible]STANCE 3RD
[illegible]	[illegible]	[illegible]	[illegible]	BURGLARY 2ND
[illegible]	[illegible]	[illegible]	[illegible]	ATT [illegible]NY - AUTO 3RD
[illegible]	[illegible] JOSE	[illegible]	[illegible]	ATT [illegible] REG VIOL-1ST OFF
[illegible]	[illegible] D	[illegible]	[illegible]	[illegible]EAP 3RD SUB 1,2,3
[illegible]	[illegible]	[illegible]	[illegible]	ATT [illegible]
[illegible]	[illegible]	[illegible]	[illegible]	[illegible] SUBSTANCE 2ND
[illegible]	[illegible] A	[illegible]	[illegible]	ATT [illegible] 1ST
[illegible]	[illegible]	[illegible]	[illegible]022	[illegible]
[illegible]	[illegible]	[illegible]	[illegible]025	[illegible] SUBSTANCE 2ND
[illegible]	[illegible]SCO	[illegible]	[illegible]022	[illegible] 1ST
[illegible]	[illegible]TON	[illegible]	[illegible]018	[illegible] CONDUCT-CHILD 1ST
[illegible]	[illegible]	[illegible]	01/22/2022	[illegible]
[illegible]	[illegible]	[illegible]	[illegible]016	[illegible] DEGREE
[illegible]	[illegible]	[illegible]	[illegible]025	[illegible]
[illegible]	[illegible]	[illegible]	[illegible]019	[illegible] 1ST
[illegible]	[illegible]	[illegible]	[illegible]	[illegible]
[illegible]	[illegible]	[illegible]	[illegible]022	[illegible]FIREARM 1ST-DEG
[illegible]	[illegible]	[illegible]	[illegible]021	[illegible]
[illegible]	[illegible]	[illegible]	[illegible]029	MURDER 2ND
[illegible]	[illegible]LYOVANY	[illegible]	[illegible]024	MURDER 2ND
[illegible]	[illegible]	[illegible]	[illegible]	ATT [illegible]EAP 2ND
[illegible]	[illegible]	[illegible]	[illegible]	[illegible]
[illegible]	[illegible]	[illegible]	[illegible]	[illegible]EAP 3RD SUB 4-8 VFO
[illegible]	[illegible] R	[illegible]	[illegible]	[illegible] DEGREE
[illegible]	[illegible]	[illegible]	[illegible]	[illegible] ACT 3RD
[illegible]	[illegible]	[illegible]	[illegible]	[illegible]
[illegible]	[illegible], MICHELE	[illegible]	[illegible]	ATT MURDER 2ND
[illegible]	[illegible]	[illegible]	[illegible]	ATT [illegible]
[illegible]	[illegible]	[illegible]	[illegible]	[illegible] DEGREE
[illegible]	[illegible] JR	[illegible]	[illegible]	ATT [illegible]
[illegible]	[illegible]	[illegible]	[illegible]	[illegible]
[illegible]	[illegible]	[illegible]	[illegible]020	[illegible]EAP 2ND
[illegible]	[illegible]TONIE	[illegible]	[illegible]022	ATT [illegible]
[illegible]	[illegible] A	[illegible]	[illegible]025	MURDER 2ND
[illegible]	[illegible]FREDDY	[illegible]	[illegible]	[illegible]
[illegible]	[illegible]	[illegible]	[illegible]	[illegible]CONTR SUB - SCHOOL
[illegible]	[illegible]THUR	[illegible]	[illegible]	[illegible] ACT 1ST
[illegible]	[illegible]ALFREDO	[illegible]	[illegible]	ATT MURDER 2ND
[illegible]	[illegible]MIGUEL	[illegible]	[illegible]	ATT MURDER 2ND
[illegible]	[illegible]	[illegible]	[illegible]	[illegible]NY - NOT AUTO 3RD
[illegible]	[illegible]	[illegible]	[illegible]	[illegible] ACT 1ST
[illegible]	[illegible]	[illegible]	[illegible]	[illegible]ER 1ST
[illegible]	[illegible]	[illegible]	[illegible]	[illegible]EAP 2ND
[illegible]	[illegible]BERT	[illegible]	[illegible]	[illegible]
[illegible]	[illegible]	[illegible]	[illegible]	ATT MURDER 2ND
[illegible]	[illegible]SAR	[illegible]	[illegible]	[illegible] SUBSTANCE 1ST
[illegible]	[illegible]DAVID	[illegible]	[illegible]	[illegible]TER 1ST
[illegible]	[illegible]	[illegible]	[illegible]	[illegible]
[illegible]	[illegible]	[illegible]	12/05/2024	[illegible]CONTR SUBSTANCE 5TH

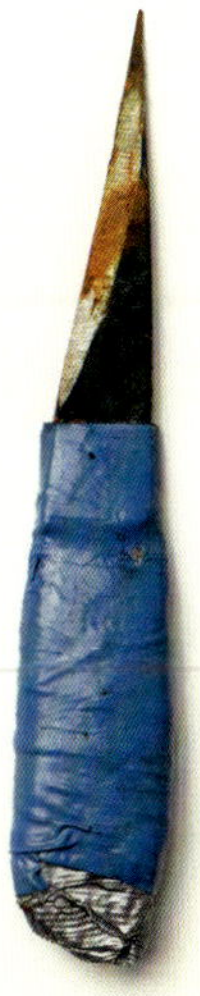

Improvised Shank, details unknown
Wawarsing, NY

DIN	INMATE NAME	LATEST ADMISSION DATE	ER DATE	CRIME
98A0256	SAWDER, BBARU	1998-01-07	06/10/2024	MHRDEAUGNDER 1ST
98A0847	DAVIZ, EMISENT	1998-01-23	09/27/2023	MURDERY2NDT
98A0982	HARNEYSTGREGORY	1998-02-03	06/28/2025	MURDER 2ND
98A0995	HADZOCKICHAURICE	1998-02-09	04/28/2023	MURDER 2ND
98A1687	REDHAKA, BANGAMIN J	1998-03-10	03/24/2024	MARDERS2ND
98A0989	MILLER, WONDEAM R	1998-03-12	03/26/2025	RAPDMYS3RD
98R2899	HANSONRIDARELL	1998-04-06	05/08/2023	MURDERY1SND
96A0873	MANGHONL, IVERHAEL	1996-04-18	05/20/2025	ATT MURDER 2ND
96A0874	DANHONY, PATRICK	1996-04-18	08/20/2022	MURDERY2NDT
96A2280	ERRIRS, GANDREW	1996-02-26	09/03/2027	KIDNAPP2ND 1ST
96A2368	STEWARLAND, MARTON	1996-05-02	05/23/2029	ROBBERY2NDT
96A2864	RABERSON, ORSAMAEL	1996-05-25	08/08/2028	BURGLARY2ND
96A2997	DAVISK, AERNK	1996-05-29	04/26/2028	CRIMEROSSDCONTR SUBSTANCE 1ST
96A3077	MHOBAS, ASSN	1996-04-29	08/17/2018	MANSLAUGHDER 1ST
96A3918	MCFARDANSUAVALENTINE	1996-03-04	08/03/2028	ROBBERY2NDT
96A3528	GRABHE, AANTON	1996-05-18	03/28/2018	ROBBERY2RND
96A3626	HOBRDEN, VADRIAN	1996-05-24	06/24/2023	MURDER 2ND
96A4442	SIERRA, DOMENGO L	1996-06-25	05/20/2021	CRIMEROSSDSTOLEN PROP 3RD
96A4641	YOUNGAMANTHONY	1996-06-28	05/07/2026	MURDER 2ND
96A4885	WENISAMKENNORN	1996-06-30	06/30/2019	BURGLARY2ND
96A5217	DAPEANGIPRAVCANTONIO	1996-07-08	08/29/2020	BURGLARY1SST
96A5929	CAMERSTNEROBERT	1996-06-24	05/26/2023	ARSON 2ND
96A6431	RAMSBERG, AMATTHEW	1996-09-03	09/25/2029	ROBBERY2NDT
96A6690	GARTALDIVIDAEL	1996-10-26	04/27/2019	MURDERS2ND
96A5785	HUMBEREEDARCHARLES	1996-02-29	09/24/2020	ATT MURDER 2ND
96A5968	RIVASU, RUDILOH	1996-10-02	05/10/2029	CRIMESALEDCONTR SUBSTANCE 2ND
96A6297	PUDHARD, ADRIAN	1996-10-08	09/20/2018	ATT MURDER 2ND
96A6798	CSORRSTUEMONTNGO	1996-11-17	04/27/2029	MURDER 2ND
96A8458	DRAWND, MHAWIDOU	1996-12-29	02/26/2024	MURDERY2NDT
95A6039	NEUCRAMS, HEABORN	1995-02-01	07/03/2024	CRIMSALESTCONTR SUBSTANCE 3RD
95A6890	ROBENSONSTEVENVIE	1995-02-25	04/23/2027	ROBBERY 2ND
95A7089	DANBRODFARIABDULKARIYM M	1995-02-29	04/29/2029	MURDERT2NDT DEGREE
95A0502	MENDOZAWOERJOSE	1995-01-18	04/29/2019	MANSLAUGHDER 1ST
95A0819	BAIREDOT, EDWARAN	1995-03-28	10/16/2021	MURDERS2ND
95A2860	BLARNZIERICATIF	1995-05-26	10/20/2020	MURDERY2NDT
95A2866	BLAROW, MRCHAEL	1995-08-04	09/16/2026	ATT MURDER 2ND
95A3028	SANCHEZ, GABARGS JR	1995-09-07	05/20/2017	MURDER 2ND
95A3129	BROOKS, ROTENEYW	1995-05-16	06/22/2028	MURDER 2ND
95A1722	AMNOR, HARRIE	1995-05-22	08/08/2029	MURDERS2ND
95A3949	ROBINA, VINTOR	1995-06-04	09/20/2024	MURDER 2ND
95A0071	RENEZ, JAANFIS	1995-06-16	07/28/2020	ROBBERY 2ND
95A0085	AHMEDYUSALEH	1995-04-09	09/30/2023	KIDNAPP2ND 2ND
95A0159	BANTY, GREGORY	1995-06-07	08/19/2022	MURDER 2ND
95A9426	MEENAMEDWARDFRERY	1995-04-27	09/26/2023	KIDNAPP2ND 1ST
95A0895	WARNER, DONNIE	1995-03-21	08/20/2026	BURGLARY2ND
95A5380	ABDNURRAHEEM, JAMES	1995-08-04	07/09/2020	ROBBERY2ND
95A6264	NAYO, KAREEM	1995-08-01	07/05/2020	MURDER 2ND
95A6652	DOVEIERASAMES	1995-08-29	04/14/2020	ATT MURDER 2ND
95A6881	DAWNSDONNSARSEY	1995-08-28	08/12/2025	MURDER 2ND
95A3276	SAUDOS, GUSBER	1995-09-08	04/13/2029	MURDER 2ND
95A6870	BARASCASTEVENSANT	1995-09-20	04/28/2018	MANSLAUGHTER 1ST
95A6417	CANCES, EVARMAR	1995-10-06	12/25/2021	ROBBERY2NDT
95A6909	DAAZOMEDOMANUEL	1995-10-27	08/06/2029	MURDER 2ND
95A8918	MAUDEEN, CRATTOHN	1995-09-05	03/06/2029	ROBBERY 1ST
95A8655	ROBBECKS, WREEBART	1995-09-25	07/25/2029	MURDER 2ND
95A8678	AGROZO, PRAVED	1995-10-20	12/29/2020	MURDER 1ST
96A0537	HOAMEN, DARRYLOPHER	1996-01-30	10/16/2027	ATT MURDER 2ND
96A6068	COEN, STEVEN	1996-02-24	06/26/2028	ATT GRAND LARCENY - NOT AUTO 2ND
96A6292	WILKEANSWIGAEAM	1996-02-29	09/02/2020	ROBBERY 1ST
96A6638	GUTIRRREZRHONAR	1996-03-09	06/08/2024	MURDER 2ND
96A6687	REDDFEN, MICHAEL	1996-03-20	08/26/2024	BURGLARY2ND
96A8866	MORSLAD, ARACHYO	1996-09-15	09/02/2026	ROBBERY2NDT
96A2853	GARCIAEIJESUS C	1996-05-22	04/05/2029	KIDNAPPING 1ST
96A2886	RUELEISPSJOSHUKEJ	1996-04-05	08/07/2028	MURDERS2ND
96A2099	SANCHEZDANIELERYMAN	1996-08-22	09/07/2019	MURDER 2ND
96A3928	MDEINAILROBERT	1996-08-27	05/29/2029	MURDER 2ND
98A0198	ARAUJO, CALVEN	1998-01-26	10/06/2026	MURDER 1ST
98A0518	YANDNE, ORLANDON	1998-01-29	03/29/2018	RAPE 1ST
98A0677	KORNOKFIJERARRYR A	1998-02-26	06/06/2023	MURDER 1ST DEGREE
98A0894	KEABROOKERICHARD	1998-02-08	01/24/2021	ROBBERY2NDT
98A6976	FAIDLNERMARONALD G	1998-12-18	12/22/2027	ATT CRIM POSS WEAP 3RD SUB 4-8 VFO
98A6709	HOMRES, ROGENN	1998-10-20	03/20/2020	ATT MURDER 2ND
98A7565	PAGANCUSHRISTIAN	1998-11-04	02/14/2027	ATT ROBBERY 2ND
98A7620	BARGHIERN, LMICHAEL	1998-11-12	10/26/2029	MURDER 2ND
98A7922	WILLIAMSDINGRESTTON	1998-12-05	10/27/2026	CRIM POSS CONTR SUBSTANCE 3RD
98A7747	YUNEG, JUNVAN	1998-12-18	02/09/2025	KIDNAPPING 1ST
98A2806	GRAENLTRONLEXANDER	1998-04-20	03/17/2018	MANSLAUGHTER 1ST
98A2761	KUMALELO, JOSEPH	1998-09-15	11/10/2023	ASSAULT 2ND
97A2057	CARIDNAMECHRISTOPHER	1997-04-24	05/24/2025	MURDER 2ND
97A2417	MARRERYTHOMASCE	1997-05-04	06/16/2025	MURDER 1ST
97A2592	WEHRNEN, MICHAEL	1997-05-08	06/14/2023	RAPE 2ND
97A2669	EDWARDS, JEREMY	1997-05-20	09/12/2029	MURDER 2ND
97A2985	CARVAROSEHERIC	1997-02-07	08/26/2024	ROBBERY 2ND
97A3436	MURAYERS, ANDREW	1997-02-20	09/20/2021	ATT BURGLARY 2ND
97A3660	MUNCKELSEFERETOON	1997-03-14	05/22/2022	CRIM SALE CONTR SUBSTANCE 2ND
97A3881	LEARKALTONSON	1997-03-24	06/25/2021	MURDER 2ND
97A5036	ZYNAM, DIANE	1997-04-07	05/08/2027	KIDNAPPING 1ST
97A5149	PERKINS, SORDELL	1997-04-21	12/26/2017	ATT MURDER 2ND
97A5497	MEYERS, CORTWAUN	1997-07-25	10/27/2019	MANSLAUGHTER 1ST
97A5737	CASANTELO, CARMINE	1997-07-26	11/11/2023	MURDER 2ND
97A5809	SIMDEOSYNDRONDRA	1997-05-27	09/05/2029	ROBBERY 2ND
97A6132	DOMINIQUE, RONALD	1997-06-14	03/27/2022	ATT MURDER 2ND
97A6296	TAERNASARFRANCISCO	1997-06-20	11/05/2023	MURDER 2ND
97A6988	RAMIRESDSJOSE A	1997-07-30	05/26/2025	MURDER 2ND

DIN	INMATE NAME	LATEST ADMISSION DATE	ER DATE	CRIME
99A6092	BOALARB, BNORICE	1999-07-20	11/18/2029	ATT BURGLARY2ND
99A6982	FERGRSON, ROMANDO	1999-07-28	06/04/2027	ATT MURDER 2ND
99A6486	DBASVO, RHAMEDOU	1999-08-29	05/26/2026	CRIM POSS WEAP 2ND
99A6829	WRABAAMS, AKABIAN	1999-10-02	07/07/2021	ROBBERY 2ND
99A6850	ROBINSONWISTERNE	1999-10-21	04/25/2021	ROBBERY 2ND
99A6286	DRAANO, PARNSAMIN	1999-10-28	04/27/2021	ASSAULT2NDT DEGREE
97A0626	FERRSTIANGLVIDGE	1996-01-18	06/28/2029	MANSLAUGHDER 1ST
97A6685	RATHGEET, KORNAN	1997-06-25	11/08/2022	MURDERS2ND
97A2861	HERURRIELMOATEECHARD D	2000-06-05	09/08/2029	ROBBERY2NDT
97A0248	HOLMAN, RAYMOND	1997-02-06	07/18/2028	ROBBERY 2ND
97A0394	SANCHEZ, MADAHAM J	1997-02-27	05/28/2018	MURDER 2ND
97A0560	MORRIS, RONSINEY JR	1997-03-26	06/03/2029	MURDER 2ND
97A1720	BYRDW, SHARRYL	1997-05-28	06/08/2021	MURDERS2ND
97A1997	HRBURAA, VJUANR	2005-06-06	09/22/2026	ROBBERY 2ND
98A2019	DANSOW, RAMFES	1998-05-08	12/23/2026	MURDER 2ND
98A2041	CARLOYURARLOS	1998-08-09	08/30/2022	KIDNAPP2ND 2ND
98A2169	SANTRASTHOMAS	1998-11-07	08/27/2022	MURDER 2ND
98A2459	URRAN, EDWARD	1998-06-27	06/08/2028	MANSLAUGHDER 1ST
98A2603	HARNIS, THOMAS	1998-05-25	02/02/2026	BURGLARY2ND
98A3190	KAANCISHEHAIN JAMES	1998-06-06	09/30/2025	ROBBERY2ND
98A3284	HKVB, KAREEM	1998-06-27	02/20/2028	BURGLARY1ST
98A3246	KOLLARR, MARRE	1999-06-20	11/10/2024	ATT MURDER 2ND
98A3559	AURRSON, PDARIEN J	1999-08-28	08/03/2025	MURDER 2ND
98A3911	SNNEDS, DANIEL	1999-05-05	12/12/2020	MURDER 2ND
98A4072	MAKIEV, SANDREW	1999-09-22	04/11/2020	MANSLAUGHTER 1ST
98A4419	BANNER, HERMANR	1999-06-08	10/20/2027	BURGLARY 2ND
98A4908	DAAZ, EDDRANCE	1999-03-16	08/06/2029	MURDER 2ND
98A4956	MACDHONS, MRATHERK	1999-07-08	11/08/2029	ROBBERY 1ST
98A5151	EDWARDSEDMARBERT	1999-07-28	12/22/2025	MURDER 2ND
98A5372	RANGED, DONALD	1999-10-04	09/25/2028	MURDER 1ST
98A5842	GRAVINDABRHISTOPHER	1999-09-08	05/08/2022	ATT MURDER 2ND
98A5615	SOTOY, STAVEN	1999-07-16	10/28/2028	ATT ROBBERY 2ND
98A6050	RAMDSANNILBARTO	1999-10-19	07/11/2026	ROBBERY 2ND
98A6587	GUTTERREZEEDMARD	1999-12-09	08/08/2024	ROBBERY2NDT
98A6588	REDDEAM, RHARAES	1999-12-20	08/26/2020	USE CHILD IN A SEXUAL PERF
98A6656	YOUNGASCORNACEY	1999-12-25	06/09/2020	ATT ROBBERY 1ST
98A6902	GANCOA, VLADYMER	1999-12-22	04/08/2025	MURDER 2ND
98A6876	ROSETN, ARONDBA J	1999-12-09	10/03/2028	CONSPIRACY 1ST
99A0653	CABERANDARIRINALD	1999-06-29	09/27/2019	MURDER 2ND
99A0866	FREEMANLTONNY	1999-02-22	10/20/2025	MURDER 2ND
99A0693	MRAUJAASJAJAHZMIN D	1999-02-05	03/26/2025	MURDER 2ND
99A0462	VARTEL, VALENTINN	1999-02-29	11/19/2029	MURDERS2ND
99A0463	MORARKA, JORRESY	1999-02-29	05/05/2027	MURDERT2NDT DEGREE
99A0884	RIODENS, KALVEN	2003-07-25	10/20/2021	MURDER 2ND
99A0890	EBERELLANAMAEL	1999-03-26	09/22/2027	ATT CRIM POSS WEAP 3RD SUB 4-8 VFO
99A1865	HORNGS, LAVBAN	1999-05-05	03/06/2025	MURDER 2ND
99A2292	CABANLINGMAREY	1999-04-09	04/30/2027	ATT ROBBERY 2ND
99A2625	MARCDIEFABDUE	1999-05-02	06/21/2029	MURDER 2ND
99A1988	RIVERASSFRANNEST	1999-06-05	04/26/2029	ROBBERY 2ND
99A1244	NUNEZ, PHAVARD R	1999-06-09	06/07/2028	MURDER 2ND
99A1786	EVARISTANTALEXANDER	1999-09-10	08/07/2028	MANSLAUGHDER 1ST
99A3792	GUBASOLDEOFRID	1999-09-28	01/14/2024	MANSLAUGHDER 1ST
99A4042	GREENJAMARK	1999-09-27	05/24/2026	MURDERS2ND
99A4595	JEFFERYSIMDRUEL	1999-05-06	04/26/2028	ROBBERY1SST
99A2592	MCCARENY, DARRICK	1999-05-08	05/16/2021	MURDER 2ND
99A4569	HOWARDOWGODERRIS	1999-08-18	05/20/2027	ATT MURDER 2ND
99A4593	NAZMARDELLBRIPASQUALE	1999-08-18	08/18/2026	ROBBERY 1ST
99A4694	MUNENGSDEANDREW	1999-05-16	11/20/2022	ATT MURDER 2ND
99A4668	BURRESON, TRAVELL	1999-05-10	09/02/2028	ROBBERY2NDT
99A5029	MITCHALEONJOHNNIE	1999-05-24	10/23/2028	BURGLARY3RD
99A5858	HYMANKITIMESRAEL	1999-09-29	05/03/2021	MURDER 2ND
99A5366	PERKENSKIMONDAVED	2004-08-27	12/09/2023	ATT MURDER 2ND
99A6037	BAKERY, ANTHAUN	1999-10-27	06/03/2017	MANSLAUGHTER 1ST
99A6794	ADAANTEXAGARMINE	1999-12-08	09/06/2028	MURDER 2ND
99A6847	RODRIGUEZELWILDON	1999-12-13	04/05/2025	ROBBERY2NDT
99A9812	DYDERIGUEZONEY	1999-12-26	12/27/2022	ATT ASSAULT2ND
99A4106	EDWARDS, FRANCISCO	2002-09-04	08/37/2022	MURDER 2ND
99A8982	DRESNES, THOMASAC	1999-09-20	08/18/2029	MURDERS2ND

FACILITY TOTAL 914

** ONLY FIRST CRIME OF COMMITMENT INCLUDED **

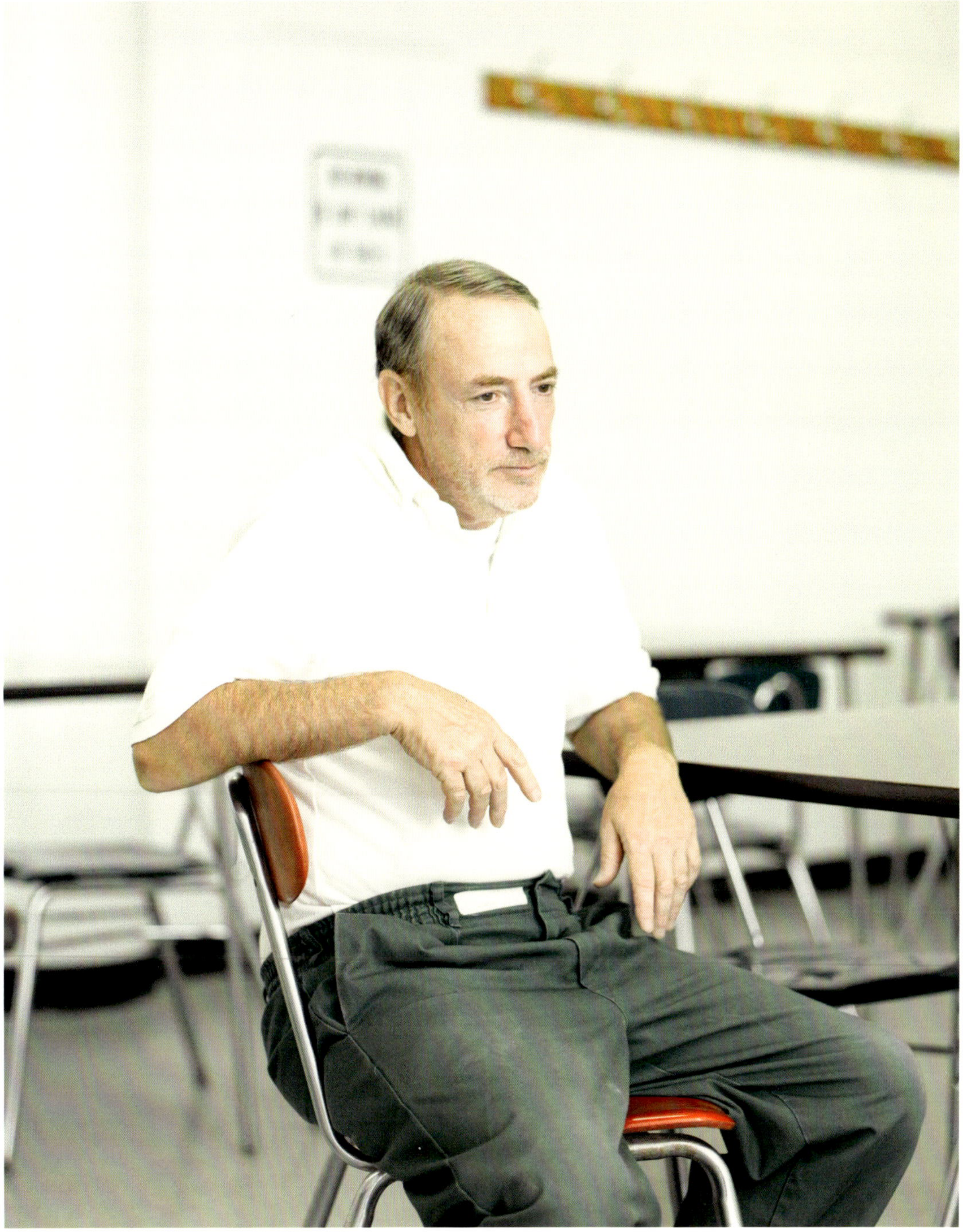

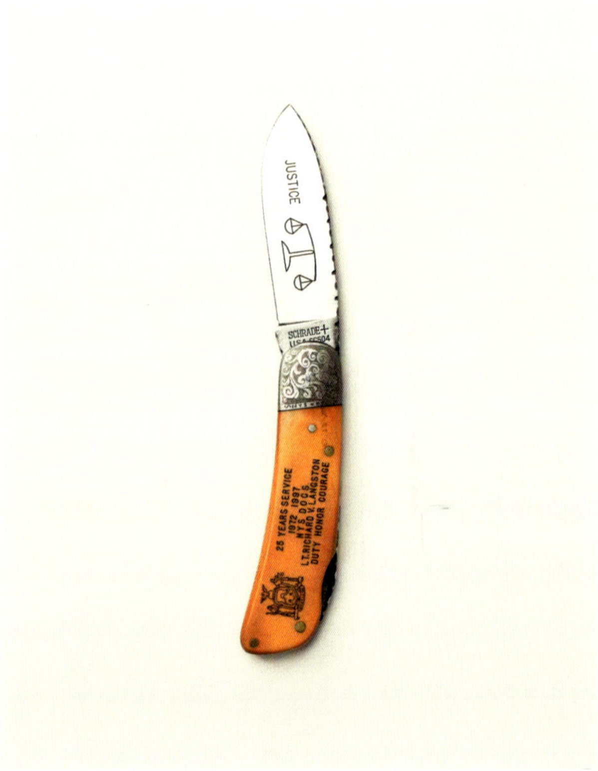

Custom Scrimshaw, 25 Years, Imperial Schrade
1997, Wawarsing, NY

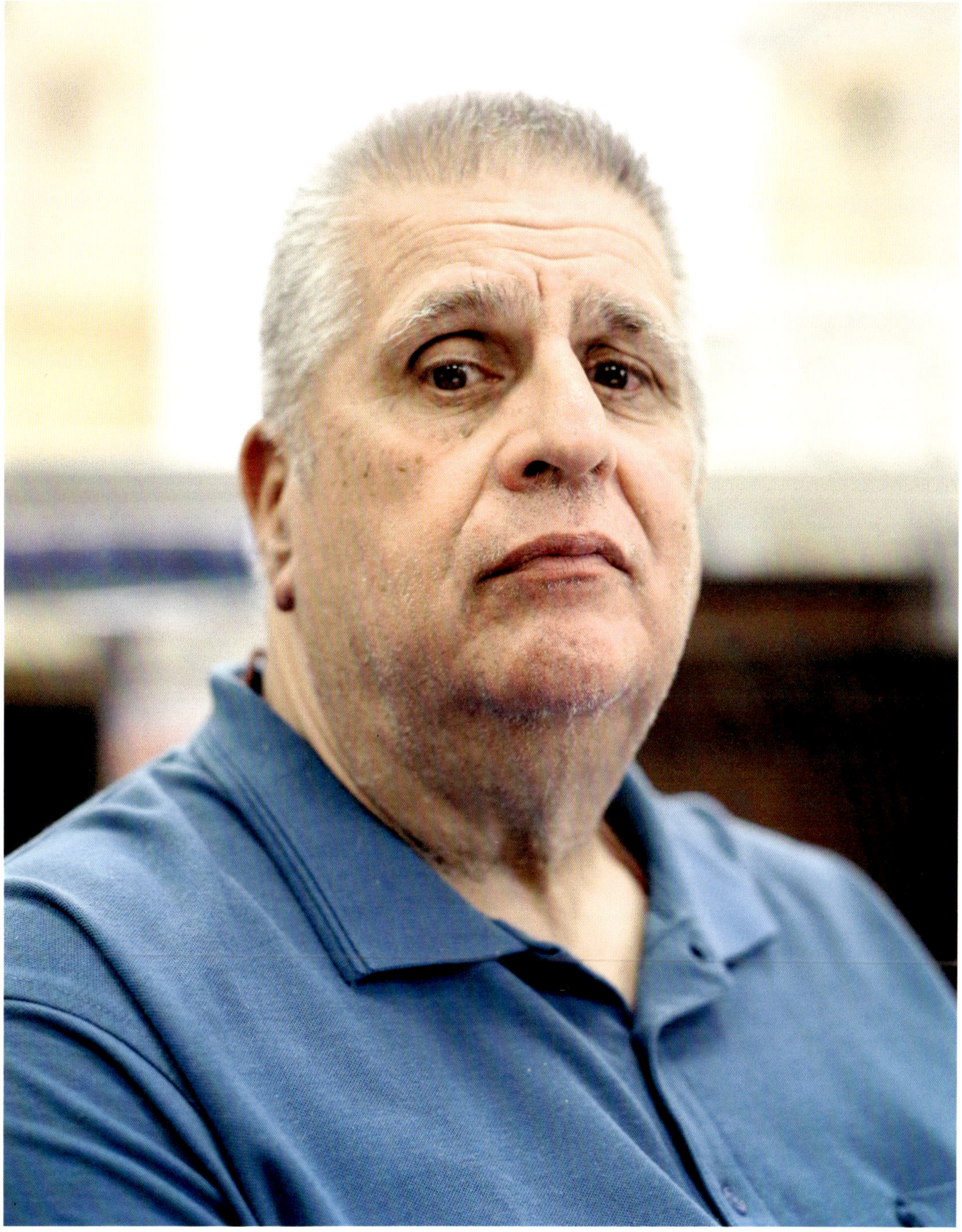

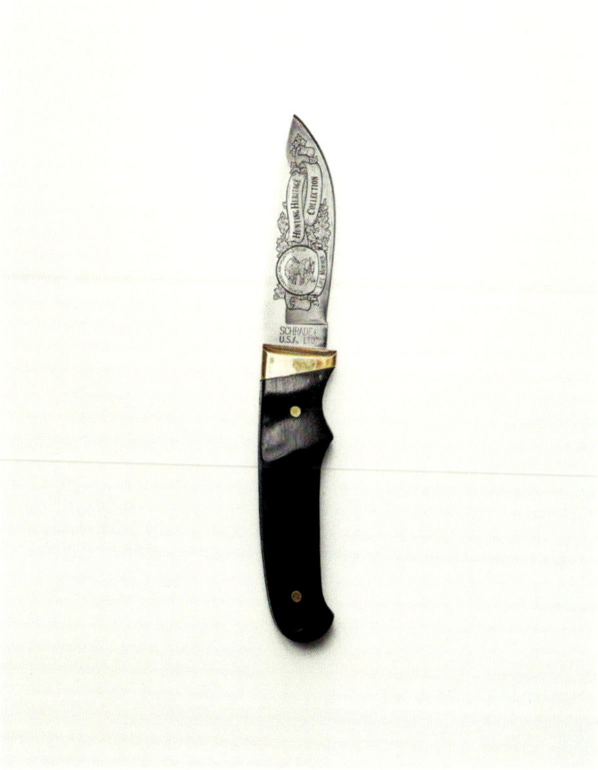

PH1 Commemorative Hunting Knife, Imperial Schrade
c. 2003, Wawarsing, NY

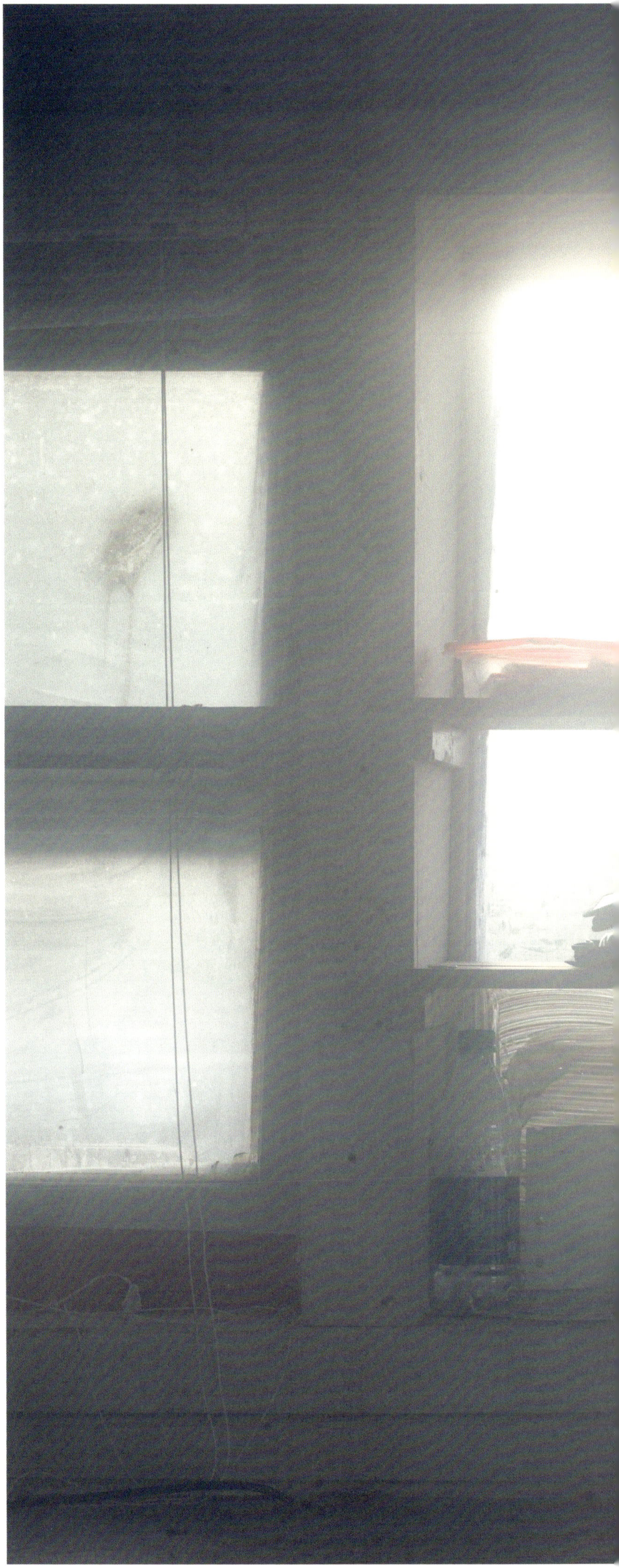

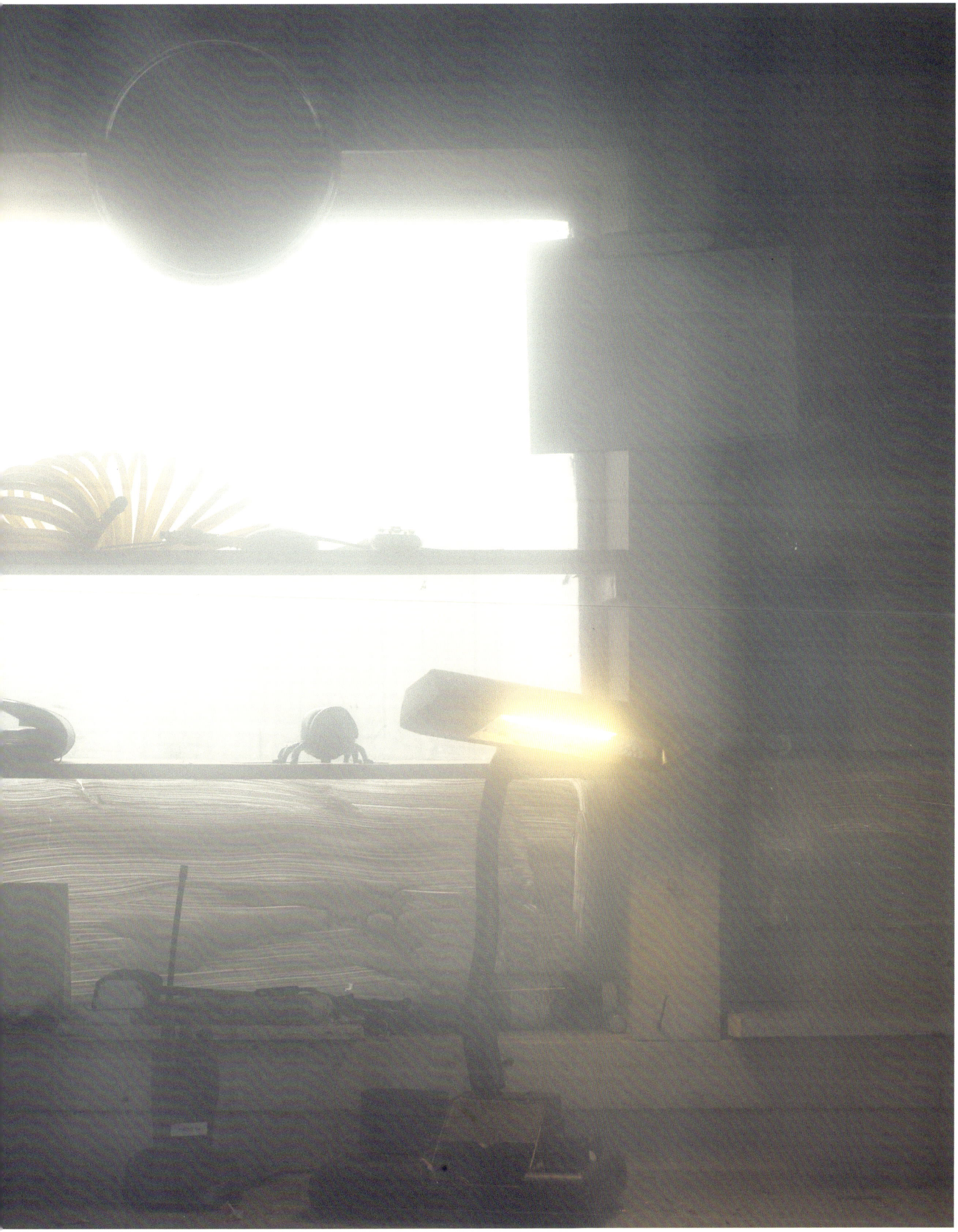

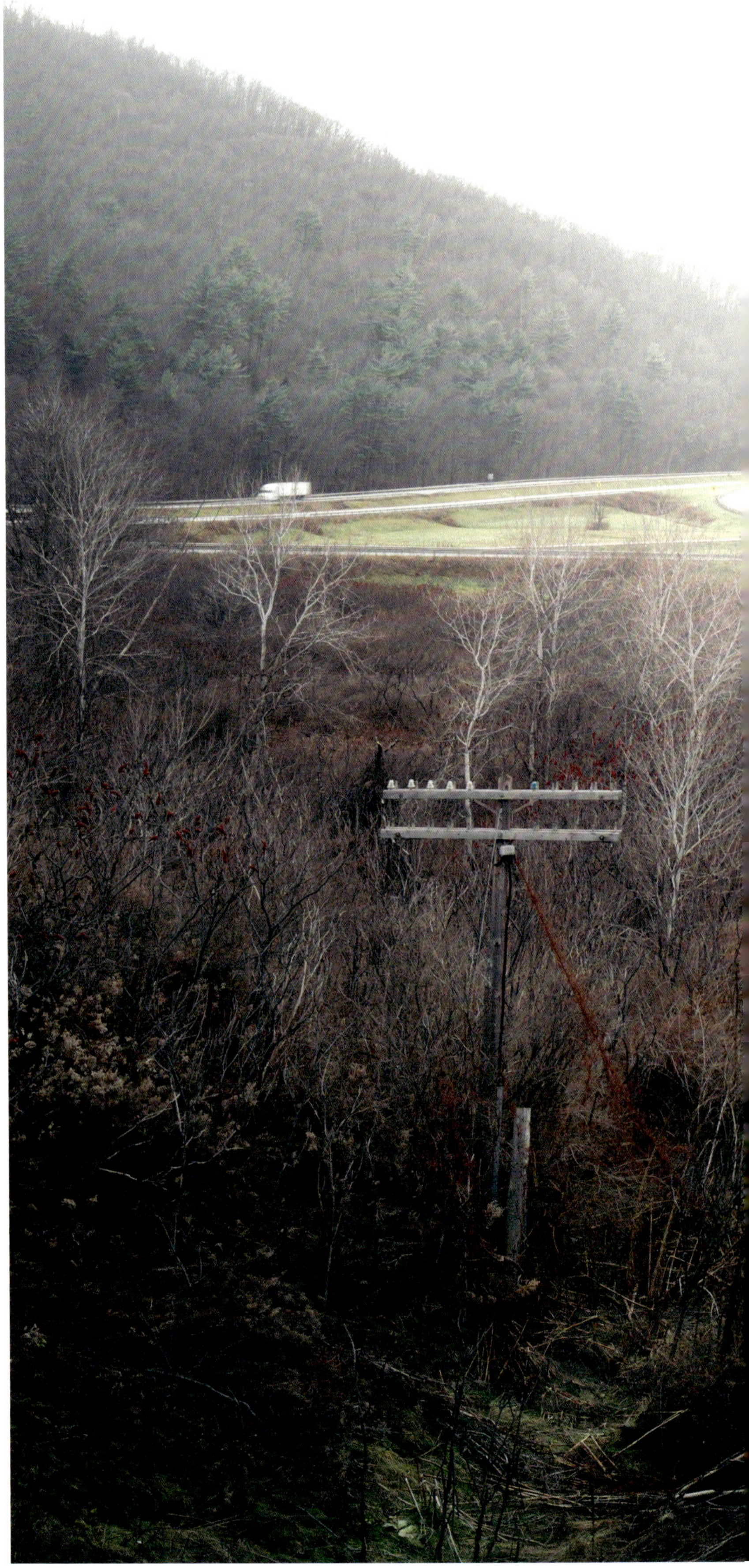

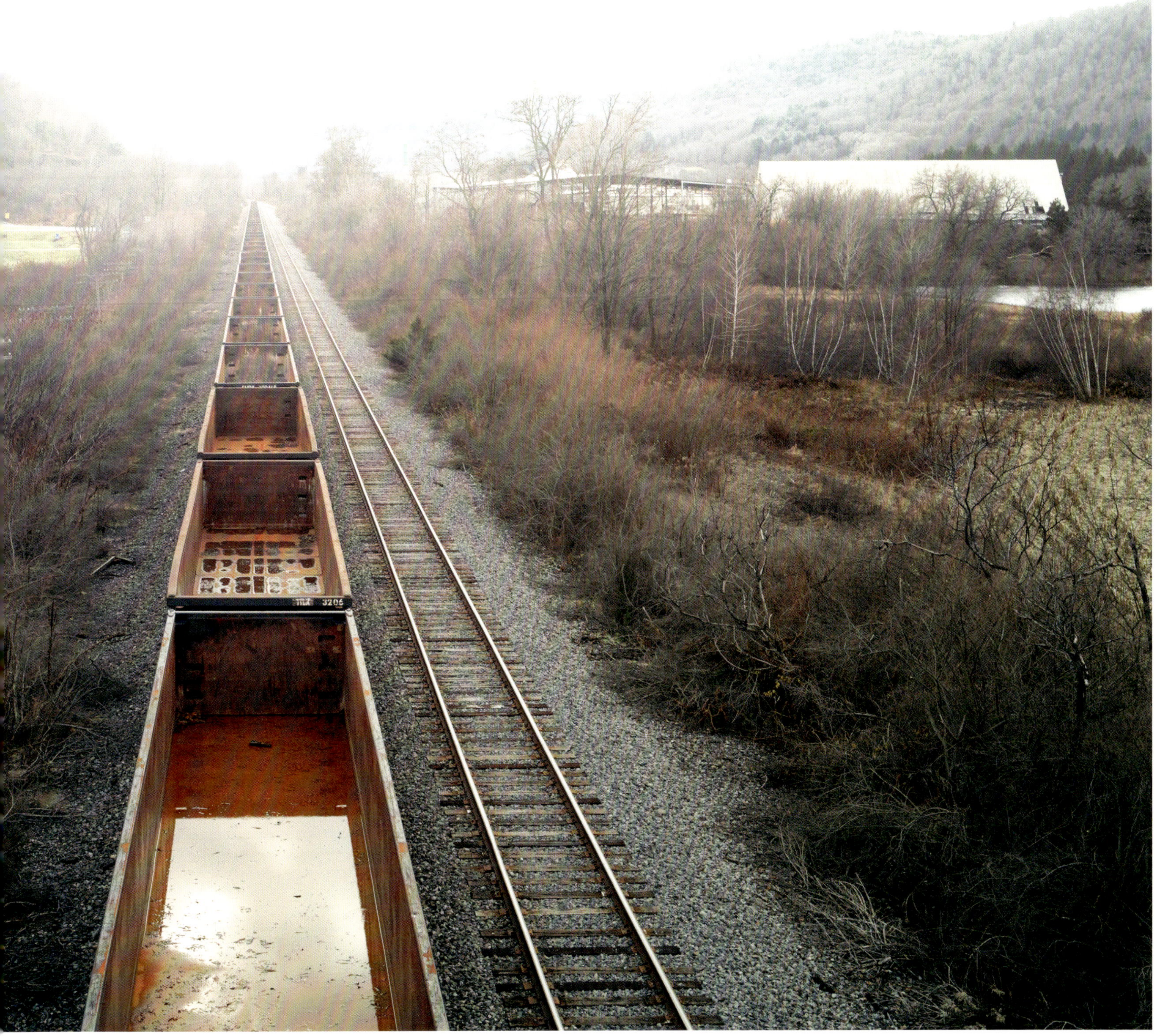

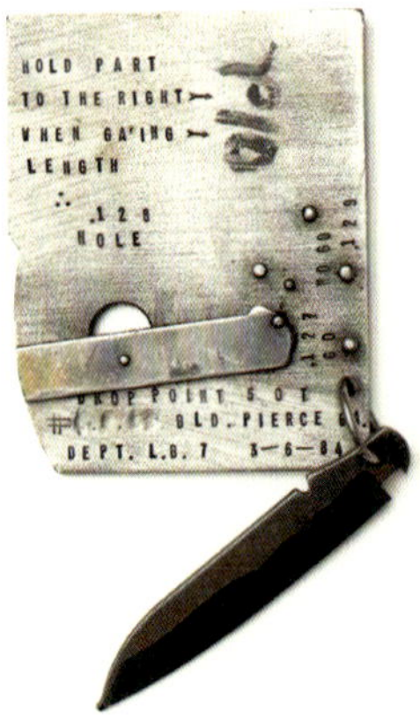

Jigging Die, Schrade-Walden
Wawarsing, NY

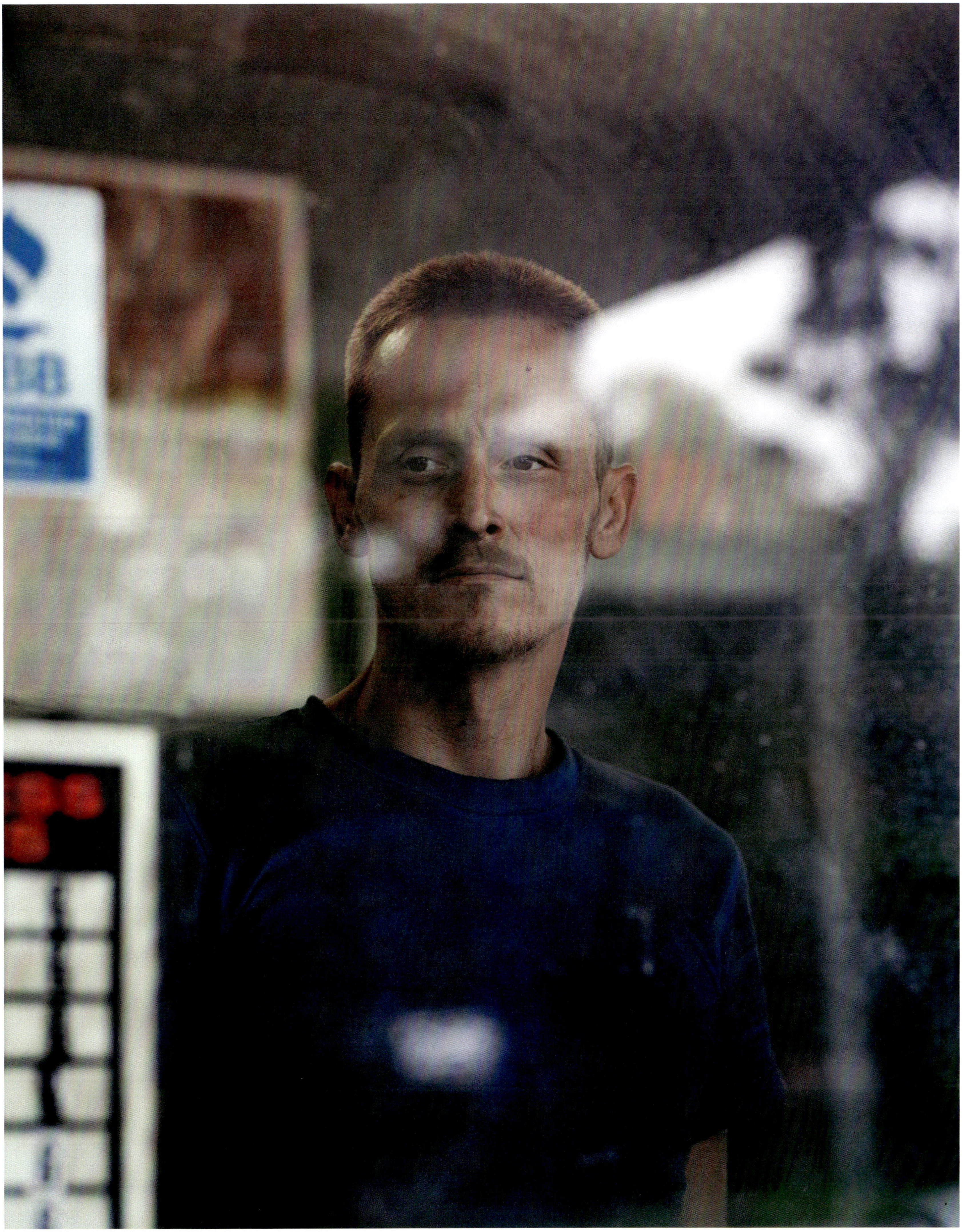

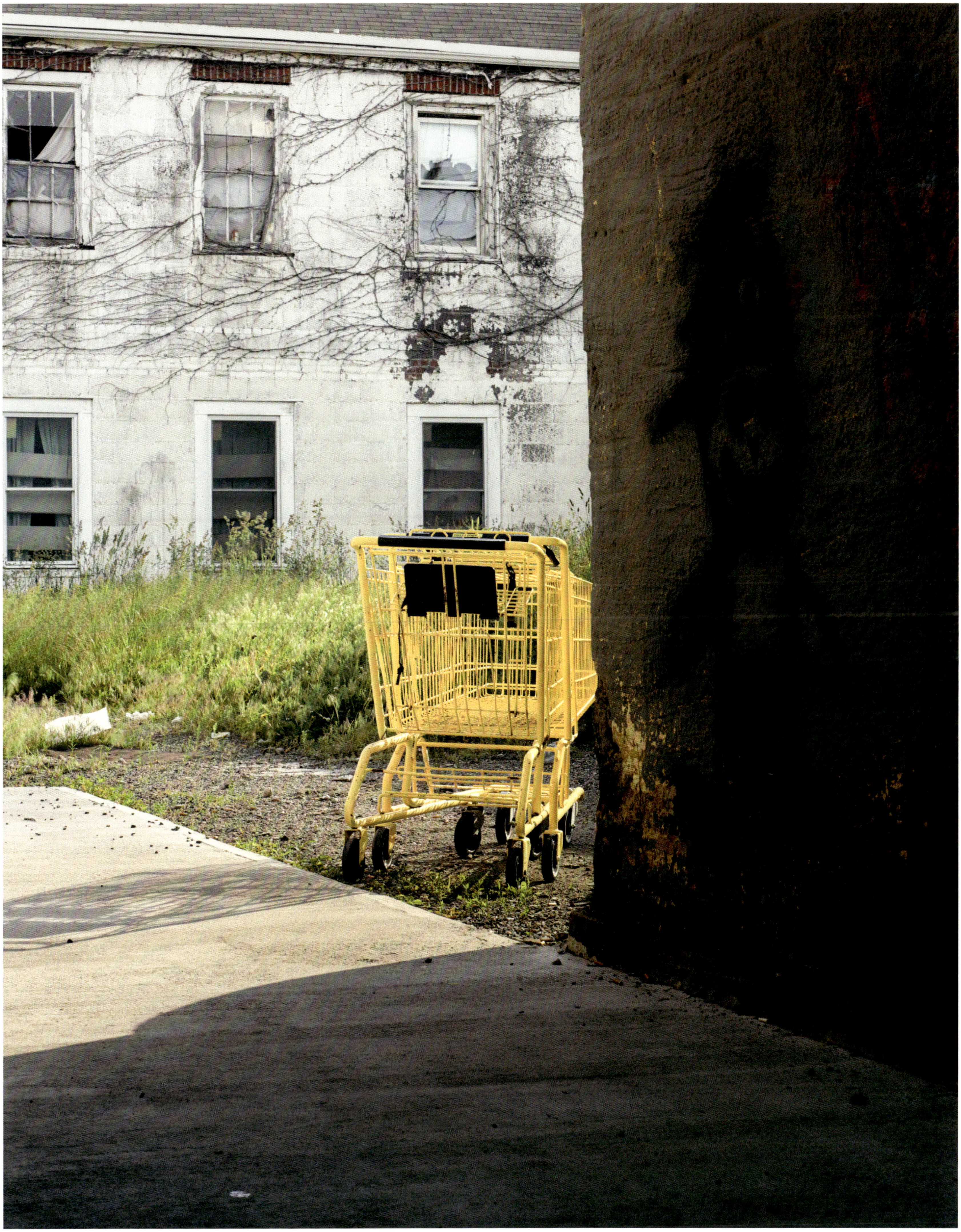

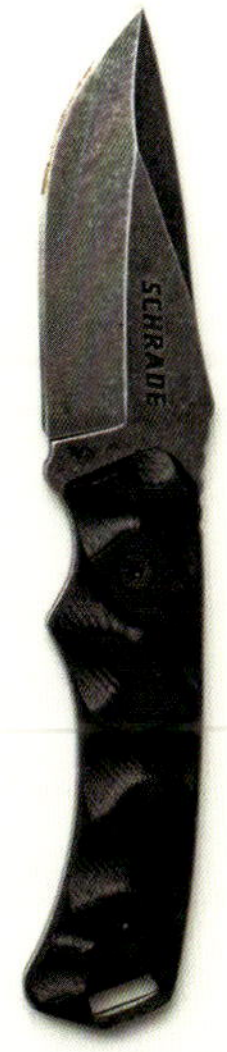

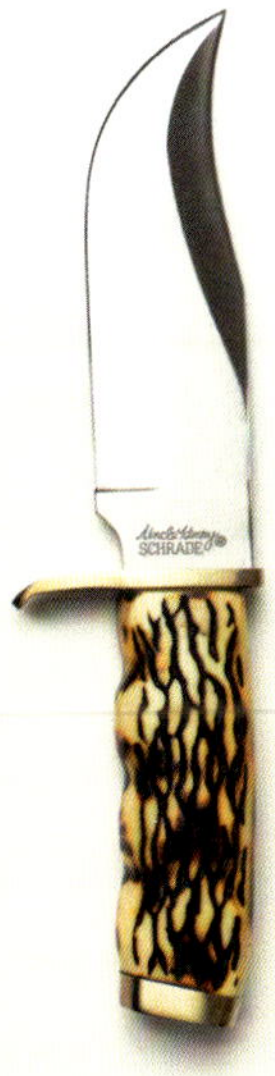

SCHF14 Drop-Point Fixed Blade
2011, Hangzhou, China

Uncle Henry Hunting Knife
2015, Hangzhou, China

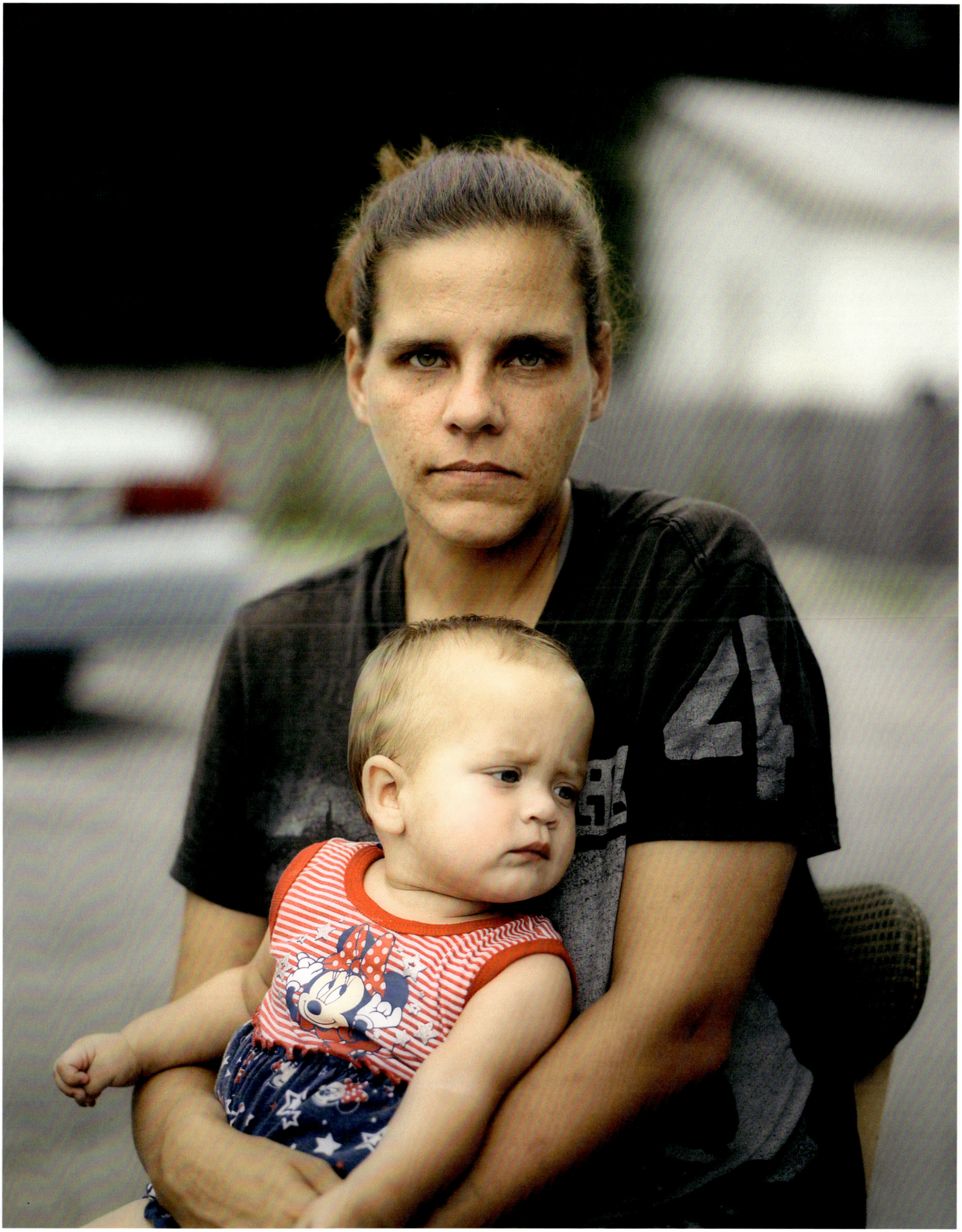

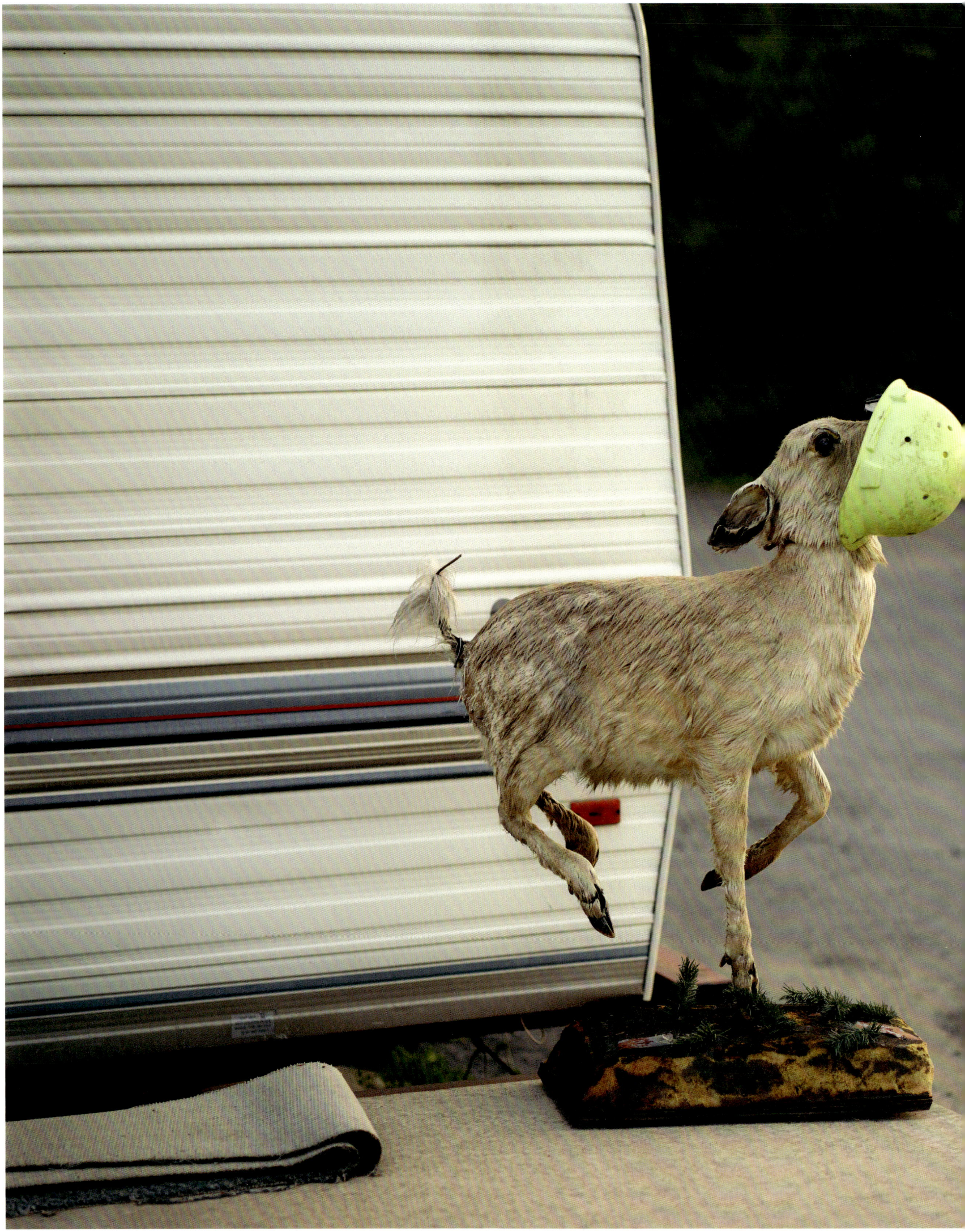

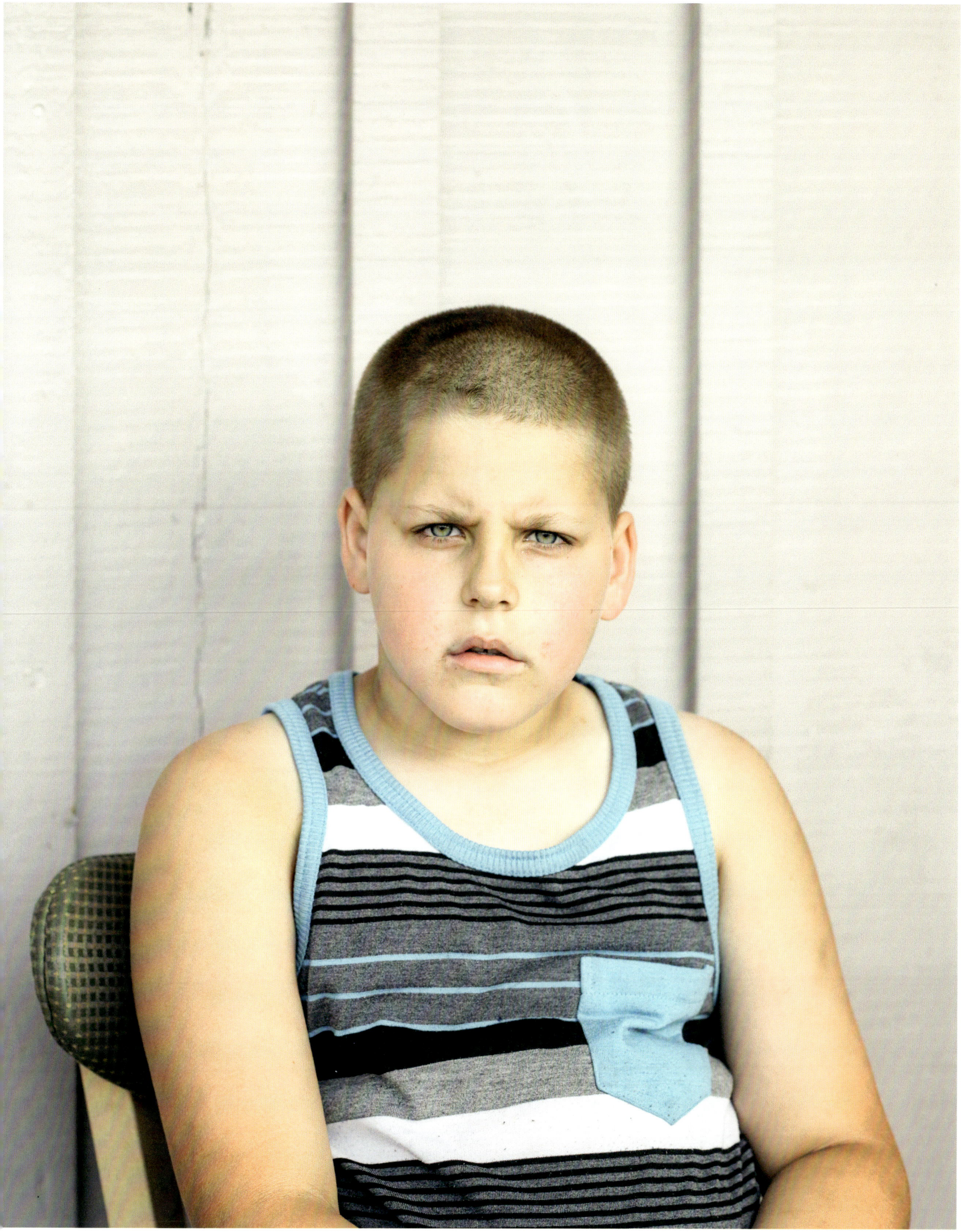

Stanley Wolukau-Wanambwa

Ruinous Silences[1]

“How can we respond to what is not presently visible, to what can never be seen within the image?”

— Eduardo Cadava[2]

Whatever it is
that keeps us from heaven,
sloth, wrath, greed, fear, could we only
reinvent it on earth
as song.

— Galway Kinnell[3]

OBSTACLES.

Is this a book that sets out to tell a story about knives? Is it a book that tells a story about the town of Wawarsing in Ulster county (pop. 13,157[4]), situated at roughly equal distances from Albany and New York city in central New York State? If you have arrived at this page in Jason Koxvold's book in chronological order, then the answer may already seem clear. The sort of story this is plainly depends on more than the elements Koxvold has marshalled in its telling—it depends upon the various changeable relationships between what the images show, and those of us now in a position to read them.

'Now' adds a crucial nuance to our sense of this unfolding interplay. To grasp the shape of the story requires reckoning with how many 'nows' orbit around these images:

There's the now of this moment—not just the moment of my writing, but the last full bloom of summer 2017. There's the now of this book's publication, and the now of your first journey through its pages. There's the now measured in the months since the inauguration of the forty-fifth president of the United States[5]. There's the now of the fourteen years since Wawarsing's standard-bearing industry shuttered its doors. There's that now of a decades-long deterioration in an already decimated industrial base—a generational now—a changeless now where diminishing economic opportunity bolsters ever-accelerating capital returns[6].

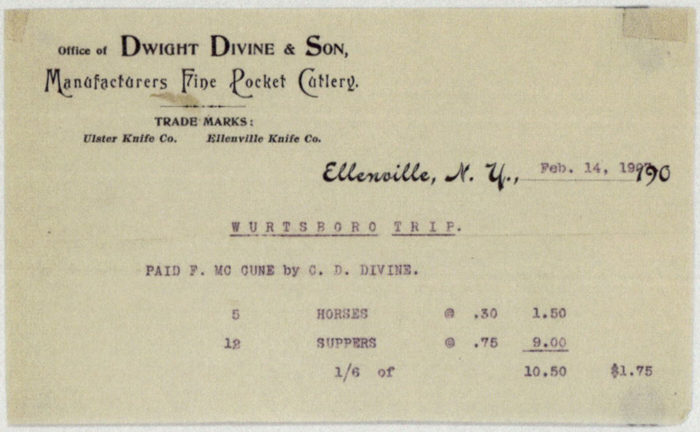

Office of DWIGHT DIVINE & SON,
Manufacturers Fine Pocket Cutlery.

TRADE MARKS:
Ulster Knife Co. Ellenville Knife Co.

Ellenville, N. Y., Feb. 14, 1907 190

WURTSBORO TRIP.

PAID F. MC CUNE by C. D. DIVINE.

5	HORSES	@ .30	1.50		
12	SUPPERS	@ .75	9.00		
	1/6 of		10.50	$1.75	

1907

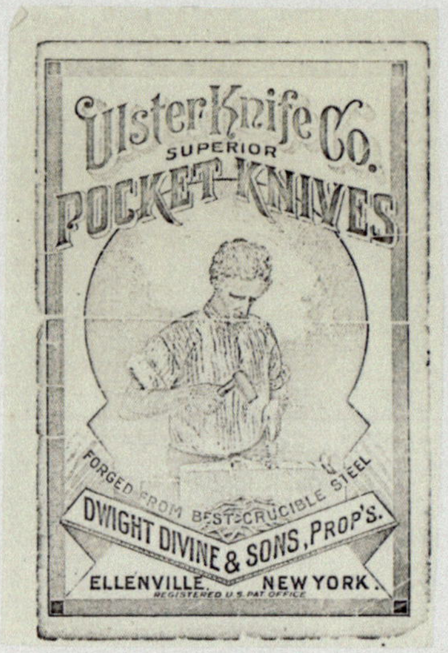

1914

There's the century-long now of a categorical inversion in the balance between the rural and the urban, in which farmers moved from being a majority of the pre-World War I population to being a dwindling minority by the turn of the millennium. There's the now of combustible and deeply fissured race relations in a country built on the systematically unequal (and too often violent) exercise of power. There's the now of single-industry towns, which is the now of fracking, the now of the maximum-security prison wage, the now of big box retail, of unattainable healthcare, the now of white collar sprawl in hospital and university towns, the now of service centres, transhipment hubs, the now of absolute dependence. I could go on...

If any of these 'nows' weighs singly in taking the measure of this work, it will invariably and disproportionately shape the book's meaning. In a moment of such profound territorial struggle in our political and social life, no fruit hangs lower than the single issue, so the question arises: how are we to look at a series of photographs made in Wawarsing in the now of late 2017?

To imagine that we might see this work outside of the parameters of a political convulsion that has tensed virtually every national sinew is as naïve as to imagine that we might each look at this work and see the same thing. The matter of *power*, inseparable from the many histories—local, national and global—of *disempowerment*, courses through these pictures, these clippings, these knives and through all the spaces in between them.

"Not since Watergate has so much uncertainty and potential disorder infected every institution, network, and power relationship"[7] writes historian Mike Davis. In aligning ourselves with or against power, in seeking recognition under the terms of its temporary embrace, we risk severing the links that bind us one to another. Kelly Oliver writes that if "recognition is conceived as being conferred on others by the dominant group, then it merely repeats the dynamic of hierarchies, privilege and domination. Even if oppressed people are making demands for recognition, insofar as those who are dominant are empowered to confer it, we are thrown back into the hierarchy of domination."[8]

We should therefore do away with any notion that those of us who read this book are in a position to confer recognition on those represented within it. Similarly, we should also do away with the notion—deeply embedded in much of the history of documentary photography—that those people shown in these pages seek anything from us as their audience. To fail at this is to risk further entrenching a set of antagonisms that have been dangerously weaponised in the very recent past.

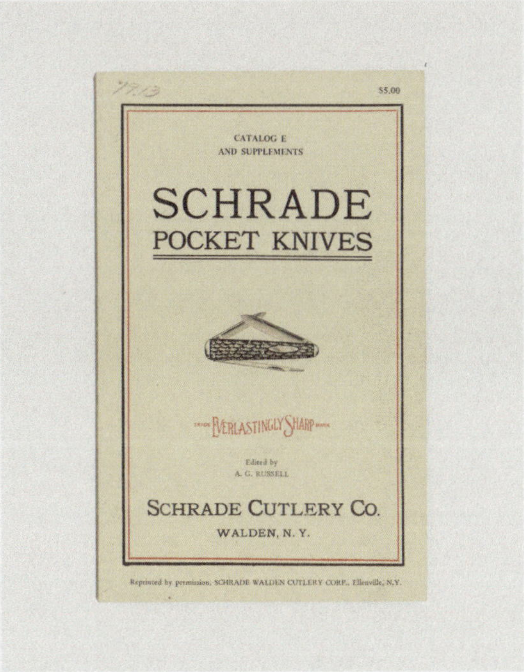

1932

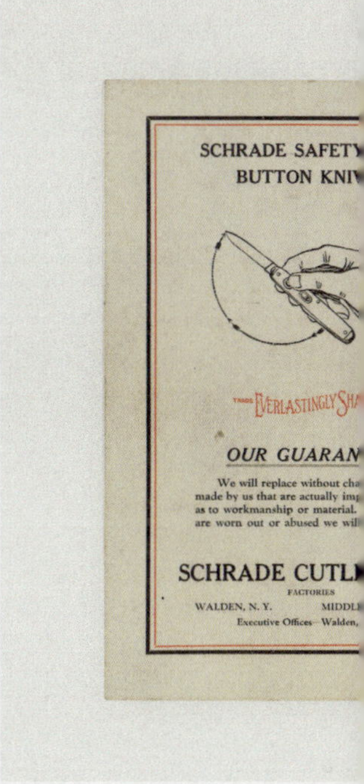

BEGINNINGS.

Koxvold gradually came to know the outlines of Wawarsing's history through the anecdotes and conversations he had with those who had lived in the town for many years, after he set out to build a home there during the recession of 2008. In late 2014, he began photographing Wawarsing in response to what he had come to know: that it has a classically American immigrant history[9]; that like much of central and upstate New York, its 19th century prospects were underwritten by the expanding economic effects of the Erie Canal; that the town's oldest—and for generations—its single largest employer, the Schrade Cutlery Corporation[10], had been founded by English immigrants in 1871; that this company formed part of a regional manufacturing hub with extensive knife-making expertise, and that this work drove the local economy for one hundred and fifty years; that on the 30th July 2004, the company abruptly and completely closed its long-foundering operations, and soon after declared bankruptcy.

The aftereffects of these events are a palpable structuring feature of the landscape, and of the changed circumstances in its communities. While, at the last, the factory took with it only 260 jobs, the rippling effects of this closure in the context of regional de-industrialisation were severe[11]. They have also proved thus far to be irreparable.

2015 Census data indicates that 83% of Wawarsing's population are of working age[12], and that 46% of those are aged between 35 and 59 years old. The Census estimates that, as of 2015, only half of Wawarsing's working age population participated in the workforce, so the 260 lost jobs represent employment for nearly one in ten of those below the retirement age who no longer work. In a town where more than one in three residents live below the federal poverty level, what seems like a little can prove more than sufficient to change everything else.

The knives in this book are thus remnants of a deep cultural history around which a sense of collective identity developed over a century and a half[13]. By opening the book with an 1886 portrait of Dwight Divine, Koxvold thus signals a continued elaboration of two parallel lineages: that of the chronological development of the town's most famous product, and that of its residents. The interweaving strands raise the questions of whether a town can be reduced to the singularity of its emblem, and what is it that remains in the wake of its dissolution?

To begin with, people. In this instance—which is to say in this work, rather than in the world from which the pictures were fashioned—what remain are preponderantly men. Men who appear to be well into, or past their middle age, and who are depicted with a consistently statuesque kind of stillness. They are generally photographed up close and within the limiting field of shallow focus, so that the extension of their arms, the weight of their bodies, the textures of the spaces that they occupy are abridged, condensed into fractional cues, which we can read out from inside the tight space that frames them.
It is tempting to elide this photographic effect with the

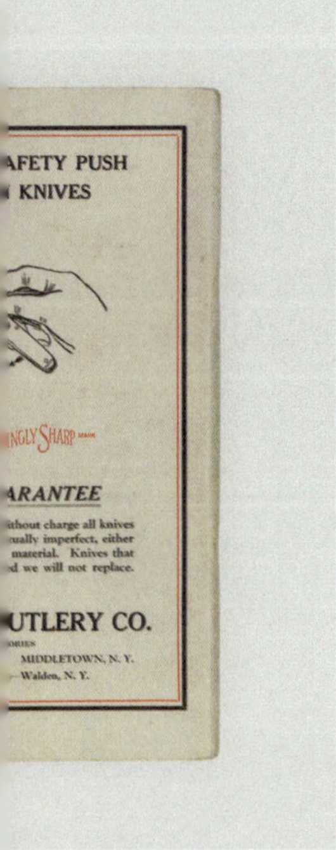

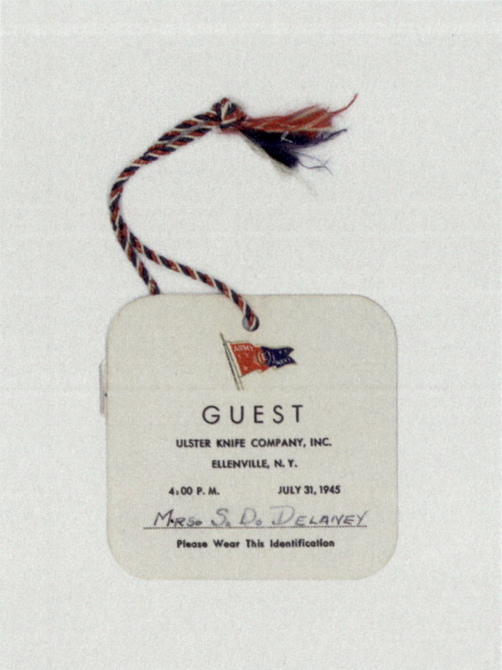

1945

overarching reality that the pictures and documents reflect. The constraints of the narrowly drawn frame heighten the intensity of minute gestures: a squint against direct sunlight, or a wide-eyed gaze in patient anticipation of the shutter seem to open up a route through the actual, through the perfunctory, toward the rich grounds of metaphor. This is the necessary deception of the photographic portrait: to confect a set of circumstances in which an appearance might rise to the surface whose genesis matters far less than its rhetorical effect.

This is to say that we should exercise some caution not to lapse into a "perceived anthropological condescension"[14] in our viewing. We should avoid any temptation to conflate the clarity of an image with a human experience we then take to be singular, solely on the photograph's terms. These men are not monoliths. While Koxvold's photographs reflect a post-industrial silence coursing through the landscape, where there is weariness in the portraits it is inseparable from the accumulated traces of a complex life.

AN IRREMEDIABLE ABSENCE.[15]

The knives shown in the book come from the Wawarsing Historical Society, in which examples from virtually every phase of the region's history of knife-making are regularly on public display. The knife museum there mirrors the double-bind characteristic of much rural de-industrialisation: it reflects the obligation to preserve in effigy that which helped to build the town—that which the town may now no longer produce, but nevertheless cannot afford to lose. Such small cities and towns too poor to be able to "leverage the hollow shells of a [once] productive economy"[16] must then lay down with their architectural ghosts, which rest in a state of decrepit inaction that looks both dated and sudden—like a solid echo.

This is a way of retaining loss. It resurfaces in much of the poetry of Galway Kinnell, whose *Last Songs* serves as an epigram for this essay and this book. In his poem *Lastness*, he writes:

> Lastness
> *is* brightness. It is the brightness
> gathered up of all that went before. It lasts.
> And when it does end
> there is nothing, nothing
> left,
>
> in the rust of old cars,
> in the hole torn open in the body of the Archer,
> in river-mist smelling of the weariness of stones,
> the dead lie,
> empty, filled, at the beginning,
>
> and the first
> voice comes craving again out of their mouths.[17]

Kinnell's rendering of our irresistible mortality is not linear but cyclical: after the end, when "there is nothing, nothing/left/in the rust of old cars (...) the dead lie,/empty, filled, at the beginning,/and the first/voice comes craving again out

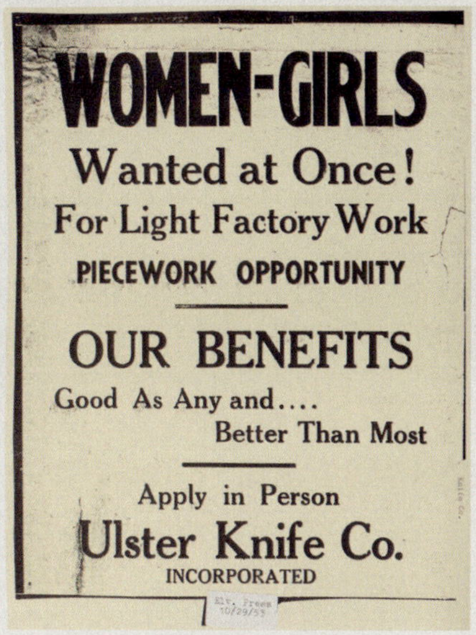

1953

of their mouths." This bears on the question of the ruin—a term that accurately defines the hollow carapace of the Schrade knife factory, which sprawls out in a picture here at the edge of town. To revisit it in pictures, within the context of the fabric of the town that surrounds it, is to reckon with the recurrence of those voices that go on sounding more than a decade after its closure.

The question of Koxvold's treatment of these ruins—the possible charge that this work represents 'ruin porn'—colours the likely reception of his work. A quick search of Google's Trend analysis tool[18] for popular search terms in the United States shows that after relatively limited use between 2004 and 2008, the phrase has steadily grown in popularity up to the present day. Beyond its immediate confirmation of the recession's effects, this data suggests a concomitant concern with how we *look* at the visible marks of the recession—marks which are themselves deeply historical, and part of a longer 'now' than the spectacle of the 2008 financial crash might encourage us to believe.

John Patrick Leary writes that "much ruin photography and ruin film aestheticizes poverty without inquiring of its origins, dramatizes spaces but never seeks out the people that inhabit and transform them," pointing to the essential role of decontextualisation in the production of the ruin's characteristic "hollow shells"[19]. The interweaving strands of the story of the knives and the present conditions of Wawarsing thus reject the romanticised melodrama of ruin porn. Koxvold has opted instead to grasp for a sense of the imbrication of past, present and future through the conjunction of economic and social life.

The photograph is both an apt and cruel method for dealing with such circumstances. It addresses the frailty and mortality of those things that it invariably outlives, but in that preservation it heightens our sensitivity to the irrecoverable moments crystallised across its vivid surfaces. We see our own ageing, our own transformation, in the mirroring encounter with the changeless elements of the photograph, even as its meanings continually shift. The photograph retains a dynamism and a persistence beyond the scope of our mortal lives, such that "the image, bearing as it always does several memories at once, is never closed," and "the *true* picture of the past is the one that is always in a state of passing away." [20]

In this way, in one of Koxvold's photographs, the congregation of green weeds pivoted toward the light of an open doorway mimic the bowed lines of the wooden wall panelling, whose grain seems to drift and droop while old living rooms, old offices, former places of work and play, surrender to a gradual rewilding whose beauty signals a cruel and irreversible reclamation. Loss and reclamation are indivisible; the present is discernible through the immanent distance of the past. Koxvold's recurrent focus on the ground in these derelict rooms, on floors fading back toward the raw condition of earth, recalls a history of illegible footsteps over and in which he steps in the making of this work.

TRACES.

In Galway Kinnell's poem *The Shoes of Wandering*, his narrator purchases a pair of second-hand shoes at the

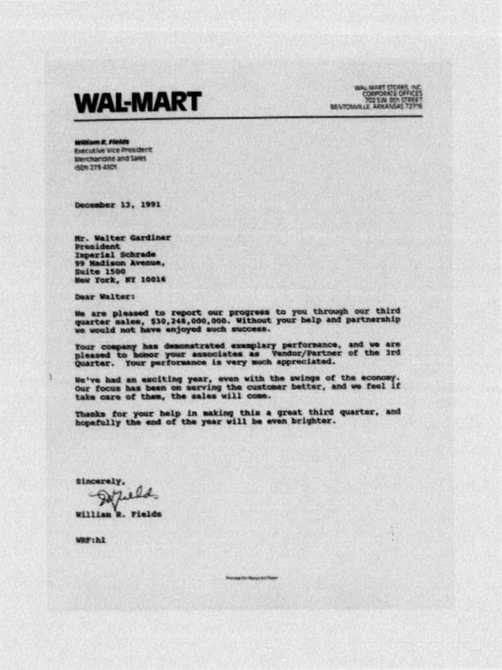

WAL-MART

WAL-MART STORES, INC.
CORPORATE OFFICES
702 S.W. 8th STREET
BENTONVILLE, ARKANSAS 72716

William R. Fields
Executive Vice President
Merchandise and Sales
(501) 273-4301

December 13, 1991

Mr. Walter Gardiner
President
Imperial Schrade
99 Madison Avenue,
Suite 1500
New York, NY 10016

Dear Walter:

We are pleased to report our progress to you through our third quarter sales, $30,248,000,000. Without your help and partnership we would not have enjoyed such success.

Your company has demonstrated exemplary performance, and we are pleased to honor your associates as Vendor/Partner of the 3rd Quarter. Your performance is very much appreciated.

We've had an exciting year, even with the swings of the economy. Our focus has been on serving the customer better, and we feel if take care of them, the sales will come.

Thanks for your help in making this a great third quarter, and hopefully the end of the year will be even brighter.

Sincerely,

William R. Fields

WRF:hl

1991

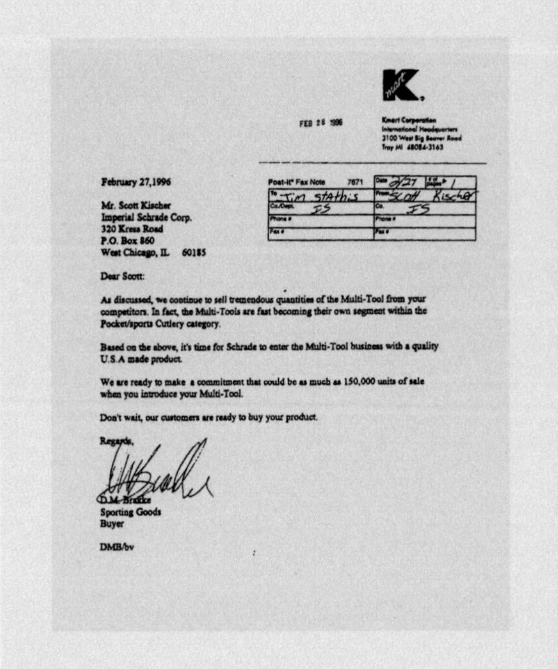

FEB 28 1996

Kmart Corporation
International Headquarters
3100 West Big Beaver Road
Troy MI 48084-3163

February 27,1996

Post-it® Fax Note 7671	Date 2/27 # of pages ▸ 1
To Jim stathis	From Scott Kischer
Co./Dept. IS	Co. IS
Phone #	Phone #
Fax #	Fax #

Mr. Scott Kischer
Imperial Schrade Corp.
320 Kress Road
P.O. Box 860
West Chicago, IL 60185

Dear Scott:

As discussed, we continue to sell tremendous quantities of the Multi-Tool from your competitors. In fact, the Multi-Tools are fast becoming their own segment within the Pocket/sports Cutlery category.

Based on the above, it's time for Schrade to enter the Multi-Tool business with a quality U.S.A made product.

We are ready to make a commitment that could be as much as 150,000 units of sale when you introduce your Multi-Tool.

Don't wait, our customers are ready to buy your product.

Regards,

D.M. Brakke
Sporting Goods
Buyer

DMB/bv

1996

Salvation Army, wears them out of the store along the streets to his hotel, sets them beside his bed before falling asleep, and finds himself at each point wrestling with the ghosts of their former owners. In "putting on, one after one,/these shoes strangers have died from, I discover/the eldershoes of my feet,/that take my feet/as their first feet, clinging/down to the least knuckle and corn." [21]

The narrator curls up on the bed, but finds that "the old/footsmells in the shoes, touched/back to life by my footsweats, as by/a child's kisses, rise", so that all of a sudden if he groans or wheezes, "it will be/the groan or wheeze of another" [22]. He is visited by dreams of the room's former residents, and by the echoing voices of the shoes' former owners. Even on waking and setting out into the streets, he finds

> each step a shock,
> a shattering underfoot of mirrors sick to the itch
> of our face-bones under their skins,
> as memory reaches out
> and lays bloody hands on the future, the haunted
> shoes rising and falling
> through the dust, wings of dust
> lifting around them, as they flap
> down the brainwaves of the te mporal road.[23]

For Kinnell, the foot may be "this lowliest/of tongues, whose lick-tracks tell/our history of errors to the dust behind,/which is the last trace in us/of wings." [24] In Kinnell's poetry, grace must be fashioned from, or uncovered in and through our repeated contact with the matter that surrounds us, even as that matter is itself seeded—better yet, suffused—with vivid traces of the past. Another reading of Warwarsing's imbrication with that past can be elaborated not only in the chronology of these knives, but also in their names.

I cannot mourn the history that produced the Allen Cutlery Company's *Nigger Chaser* knife, shown earlier in the pages of this book. Nor can I disregard the haunting presence of that history in this work. The tremendous utility of these goods to the US government (and its many citizens) since the mid-nineteenth century all but guarantees that such implements—designed for hunting, tree-scoring, spudding, skinning and pruning—also scored and pierced the black flesh of American citizens, irrespective of the impetus of a given knife's name. They are tools designed for specific uses, but their utility does not end with the completion of routine tasks: they are also phallic symbols of American male virility and danger, latent or explicit threats of incipient male violence. Some pride in this lingers on in their aspect, and in their names.

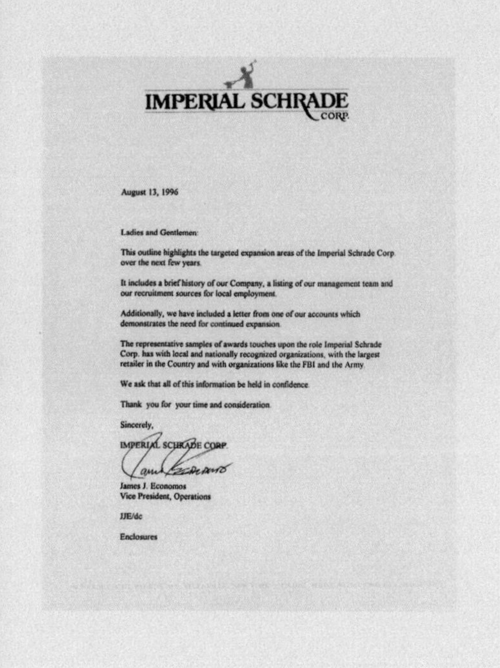

IMPERIAL SCHRADE CORP.

August 13, 1996

Ladies and Gentlemen:

This outline highlights the targeted expansion areas of the Imperial Schrade Corp. over the next few years.

It includes a brief history of our Company, a listing of our management team and our recruitment sources for local employment.

Additionally, we have included a letter from one of our accounts which demonstrates the need for continued expansion.

The representative samples of awards touches upon the role Imperial Schrade Corp. has with local and nationally recognized organizations, with the largest retailer in the Country and with organizations like the FBI and the Army.

We ask that all of this information be held in confidence.

Thank you for your time and consideration.

Sincerely,

IMPERIAL SCHRADE CORP.

James J. Economos
Vice President, Operations

JJE/dc

Enclosures

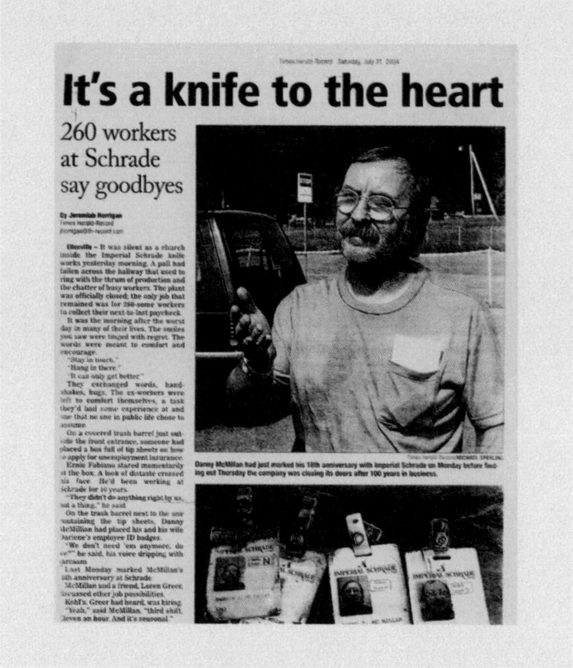

Times Herald-Record Saturday, July 31, 2004

It's a knife to the heart

260 workers at Schrade say goodbyes

By Jeremiah Horrigan
Times Herald-Record

Ellenville – It was silent as a church inside the Imperial Schrade knife works yesterday morning. A pall had fallen across the hallway that used to ring with the thrum of production and the chatter of busy workers. The plant was officially closed; the only job that remained was for 260-some workers to collect their next-to-last paycheck.

It was the morning after the worst day in many of their lives. The smiles you saw were tinged with regret. The words were meant to comfort and encourage.

"Stay in touch."

"Hang in there."

"It can only get better."

They exchanged words, handshakes, hugs. The ex-workers were left to comfort themselves, a task they'd had some experience at and one that no one in public life chose to assume.

On a covered trash barrel just outside the front entrance, someone had placed a box full of tip sheets on how to apply for unemployment insurance.

Ernie Fabiano stared momentarily at the box. A look of distaste crossed his face. He'd been working at Schrade for 10 years.

"They didn't do anything right by us, not a thing," he said.

On the trash barrel next to the one containing the tip sheets, Danny McMillan had placed his and his wife Darlene's employee ID badges.

"We don't need 'em anymore, do we?" he said, his voice dripping with sarcasm.

Last Monday marked McMillan's 18th anniversary at Schrade.

McMillan and a friend, Loren Greer, discussed other job possibilities. Kohl's, Greer had heard, was hiring.

"Yeah," said McMillan, "third shift. Seven an hour. And it's seasonal."

Danny McMillan had just marked his 18th anniversary with Imperial Schrade on Monday before finding out Thursday the company was closing its doors after 100 years in business.

2004

So too do Schrade's ties to prisons linger in the panoply of knives, as in the commemorative *Barlow Scrimshaw* knife from 1983, or in the *Custom Scrimshaw* knife awarded for 25 years of service as a prison guard, or in the rusted devilish tip of the *Improvised Shank* (details unknown). These knives were intended for use within the opaque interiors of the two correctional facilities that squat in the centre of town. Given the subsequent disassembly of Schrade—given its dismemberment by de-industrial pressures—these knives seem symptomatic not only of structural economic decline, but of a male tradition whose symbolism has lost much of its once-vaunted vigour (although little of its lethal capacity).

In the elision of images of the prison, readouts of its inmates and images of these knives, Koxvold's work threads together lassitude, ceremonial stillness and rigid order with incarceration and rehabilitation. At least, that must be the hope: that past violences are foresworn and new possibilities cultivated in a town whose losses equal those of many of the prison's inmates. The prison layers loss onto a landscape shaped by its generational imprint. While it offers employment for some, and economic opportunity for those serving inmate's families, it nevertheless reiterates a logic of reduction, retrenchment and repression, which bonds the inmates to the knives, and which bonds those two in turn to the town.

That knives with these histories, once the fulcrum of the lifework of this region, are now a glowering absence in this small town—its trademarks auctioned off in the firesale of bankruptcy—redoubles symbolic (and actual) violence back on the inhabitants who live in its wake. The demise of Schrade is, in this sense, also a profound mark of emasculation, and while its effects are plainly indifferent to the gender of their victims, Schrade's cessation, its degradation, represents a cut into the psyche that may not heal for generations.

NEW BEGINNINGS.

Beyond the litany of personal conversations and local news stories, the loss of Schrade has been discussed and debated online for many years. The contextual factors have been wrung for any salient and overlooked detail. The chronology of events has been rehearsed and re-rehearsed. In a forum titled "Prologue at the Funeral" from March 2006, a commenter named "relodr36" cuts to the heart of it all:

> "A lot of this off-shoring is being justified in the name of "share-holder value". The CEO's,etc.,are sure raking in big money while they're also closing pension plans."[25]

Another commenter named "lt632ret" remarks that "my only problem was dealing with a government which has sworn our extinction." It is hard to argue with the fundamental accuracy of such claims in 2017. Obsolescence is tremendously profitable, and at a federal level, the fate of post-industrial regions is more a political than an economic concern.

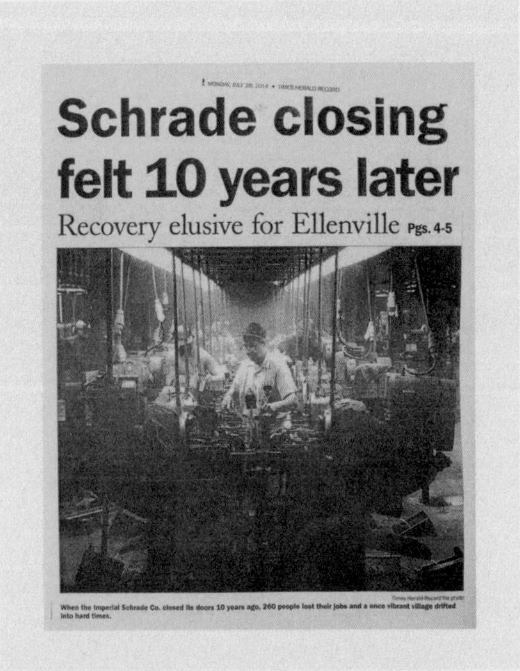

MONDAY, JULY 28, 2014 • TIMES HERALD-RECORD

Schrade closing felt 10 years later

Recovery elusive for Ellenville **Pgs. 4-5**

Times Herald-Record file photo

When the Imperial Schrade Co. closed its doors 10 years ago, 260 people lost their jobs and a once vibrant village drifted into hard times.

2014

Nevertheless, it is hard to swallow the recurrence of racist vitriol in these forums, as it arises in and among the many lucid critiques of regional neglect. The sheer frequency and spread of factory closings, the number of intimate friends and co-workers affected, the sums of debt and sales and profit and loss, the depth of the jobless abyss that follows on the heels of this devastation: these are phenomena whose enormity can bring contextual thinking to a standstill, opening the door for phantom Others to be pressed into remedial service. But it would be naïve to presume that this animus has a singular cause, much less a single historical origin.

Despite a 50% jobless rate, Wawarsing's story did not end with the closing of the Schrade factory. As Jeremiah Horrigan wrote on the tenth anniversary of the closing:

> "The workers from Schrade? They have moved on — to other places or other jobs and other lives. To where? How many? Are they OK? No one seems to know exactly. No one has tracked them. (...) The village — the entire community — has moved on too. It has gone all-in on casino gambling as the answer to its decades-long decline." [26]

Beyond this ultimately unsuccessful venture, the town has come to depend upon employers such as Wal-Mart, local healthcare providers, and two correctional facilities. But a dependence on state funding for correctional institutes premises economic survival on the mass incarceration of others. Such a need may well (quite logically) translate into a deepening political commitment to the ongoing war on the poor, the black and the brown (otherwise known as the Drug War). I think here of lines from Richard Hugo's famous poem *Degrees of Gray in Philipsburg*, where his narrator reminisces in the shadow of "two stacks high above the town,/two dead kilns, the huge mill in collapse/ for fifty years that won't fall finally down." [27] He asks:

> Are magnesium
> and scorn sufficient to support a town,
> not just Philipsburg, but towns
> of towering blondes, good jazz and booze
> the world will never let you have
> until the town you came from dies inside? [28]

In the absence of a unifying narrative that bonds the residents—indeed the region—at its very core as manufacturing once did, in the absence of those working men and women, and of that constructive labour, what fills the void in the aftermath collapse? Gambling and crime? Casinos and prisons? Addiction on all sides of an equation in which genuine effort and expertise are mobilised around the ceaseless production of loss?

It might be better to turn back to those faint footsteps, and to spend a while listening for ghosts.

1 Eduardo Cadava ""Lapsus Imaginis": The Image in Ruins" OCTOBER Vol. 96 (Spring 2011) p. 36

2 Eduardo Cadava ""Lapsus Imaginis": The Image in Ruins" p. 41

3 Galway Kinnell "Last Songs" Body Rags [Boston: Houghton Mifflin Co, 1968]

4 A figure that likely includes a prison population of approximately 1,200 inmates

5 Who reportedly lost Ulster County in the 2016 election by just shy of a 10% margin: http://www.politico.com/2016-election/results/map/president/new-york/ (Last accessed: 31st July 2017)

6 As a commenter with the handle "relodr36" on the Schrade Knives Collectors forum observes: "A lot of this off-shoring is being justified in the name of "share-holder value". The CEO's,etc.,are sure raking in big money while they're also closing pension plans." BladeForums.com, "Prologue at the Funeral" http://www.bladeforums.com/threads/prologue-at-the-funeral.394611/ (Last accessed: 1st August 2017)

7 Mike Davis "The Great God Trump and the White Working Class" Catalyst: A Journal of Theory and Strategy, Vol. 1 No. 1 (Spring 2017) https://www.jacobinmag.com/2017/02/the-great-god-trump-and-the-white-working-class/ Originally published in Jacobin, 7th February 2017 (Last accessed: 31st July 2017)

8 Kelly Oliver Witnessing: Beyond Recognition [Minneapolis: University of Minnesota Press, 2001] p. 9

9 Built on British colonial expropriation of indigenous populations in the 18th century.

10 Later known as Imperial Schrade Corporation

11 Nearby competitor Camillus, in Syracuse, NY, declared bankruptcy two years later in September 2006.

12 Above sixteen years of age.

13 As Jeremiah Horrigan writes in the Times Herald Record: "Schrade was more than a job. (...) And what the men and women of Ellenville made there was special. And it was something you could hold in your hand, a gift handed down through the generations, something many sons of Ellenville carry with them to this day. The workmanship the company demanded and got from its workers was the bulwark that allowed it to thrive in competition with other domestic knife-makers like Camillus and Gerber and Case." Jeremiah Horrigan "Ellenville's anniversary of sadness"

14 Mike Davis "The Great God Trump and the White Working Class"

15 Galway Kinnell "Last Songs"

16 John Patrick Leary "Detroitism" Guernica magazine, January 15th 2011 https://www.guernicamag.com/leary_1_15_11/ (Last accessed: 31st July 2017)

17 Galway Kinnell "Lastness" The Book of Nightmares [Boston: Houghton Mifflin Company, 1971] pp. 71 – 75

18 https://trends.google.com/trends/explore?date=all&q=ruin%20porn (Last accessed: 31st July 2017)

19 John Patrick Leary "Detroitism"

20 Eduardo Cadava "'Lapsus Imaginis': The Image in Ruins" p. 41

21 Galway Kinnell "The Shoes of Wandering" The Book of Nightmares, p. 19

22 Galway Kinnell "The Shoes of Wandering" p. 20

23 Galway Kinnell "The Shoes of Wandering" p. 21

24 Galway Kinnell "The Shoes of Wandering" p. 21 – 22

25 BladeForums.com, "Prologue at the Funeral"

26 Jeremiah Horrigan "Ellenville's anniversary of sadness" Times Herald Record, 27th July 2014 http://www.recordonline.com/article/20140727/NEWS/407280319 (Last accessed: 1st August 2017)

27 Richard Hugo "Degrees of Gray in Philipsburg" Making Certain It Goes On: The Collected Poems of Richard Hugo [New York: W. W. Norton and Company Inc., 2007] p. 216

28 Richard Hugo "Degrees of Gray in Philipsburg" p. 217

For my son, Finn Leif Koxvold.

I owe a debt of thanks to Stanley Wolukau-Wanambwa, Brian Ulrich, Shane Rocheleau, Sean Stewart, Timothy Briner, Shane Lavalette, Andrew Miksys, Kalpesh Lathigra, Daniel Shea, Lewis Chaplin, Jos Morree, Franca Koxvold, John Mannion and Amrita Stützle at Light Work, and my wife Suzi, without whom this book would not have been possible.

Special thanks to Rich Langston and the Wawarsing Historical Society for granting access to their collection of knives, the New York State Department of Corrections, and the Ellenville Public Library for their assistance in the researching of this project.

Edition of 750
First published in 2017 by Gnomic Book
ISBN 978-0-9985180-2-2

Printed in The Netherlands
Production by Jos Morree FINE BOOKS

www.koxvold.com
www.gnomicbook.com

Gnomic
Book